MAKING THE MOST OF

OFFICE 2000

FOR IBT III

ANGELA BESSANT

Heinemann Educational Publishers,
Halley Court, Jordan Hill, Oxford OX2 8EJ
A division of Reed Educational & Professional Publishing Ltd

Heinemann is a registered trademark of Reed Educational & Professional Publishing Limited

OXFORD MELBOURNE AUCKLAND JOHANNESBURG BLANTYRE GABORONE
IBADAN PORTSMOUTH NH (USA) CHICAGO

First published 2001
2003 2002
10 9 8 7 6 5 4 3 2

A catalogue record for this book is available from the British Library on request.

ISBN 0 435 45546 X

Designed by Wendi Watson

Typeset by TechType, Abingdon, Oxon

Printed and bound in Great Britain by Thomson Litho Ltd, East Kilbride, Scotland

Screenshots reprinted with permission from Microsoft Corporation

Acknowledgements
Producing a book is always a team effort. Thanks are due to Gillian Burrell and Pen Gresford at Heinemann, and to my daughter, Gemma, for all their hard work on this edition.

Angela Bessant
www.bessant.co.uk

Contents

Introduction

This book covers the syllabus for the OCR/RSA Integrated Business Technology (IBT) Level III qualification, but it would be equally useful for anyone wanting to advance their skills in Microsoft Office 2000. It assumes competence in Microsoft Office 2000 to OCR/RSA IBT Level II (this includes word processing, spreadsheet, database, graphical representation and integration skills) and is the natural progression from the book *Learning to Use Office 2000 for CLAIT and IBT II*. The quick reference guides at the end of chapters will serve to refresh topics that were covered in detail in the aforementioned book.

The disk accompanying this book contains files for practice exercises and assignments that will be used to demonstrate skills step by step, together with files for the Full Practice Assignment given in Part 2.

Part 1 covers and revises skills required for success in this qualification.

Part 2 contains a Full Practice Assignment.

Also included are the syllabus for IBT III, specimen answers to the exercises and an appendix containing hints and tips and forms for you to complete as you work through the assignments.

The RSA IBT III scheme

For the RSA IBT III qualification candidates need to demonstrate competence in the following areas (applications used in this book are given in brackets).

- Electronic communications (Outlook Express 5)
- File management (Windows 98 Explorer)
- Source data processing (Access 2000 and Excel 2000)
- Automated presentation production (PowerPoint 2000)
- Publication production (Word 2000) (You may prefer to use a desktop publishing (DTP) application eg Microsoft Publisher for the publication production.)

You are given a scenario together with accompanying files and tasks that need to be completed in a certain time limit.

This book covers all the skills necessary to gain competence at this level. Part 1 is broken down into chapters which concentrate on each application program in detail, giving step-by-step guidance, practice and quick reference guides. The examples and exercises are based around the scenario, 'Naturetrail Holidays' (see below). The same scenario is the basis for the Full Practice Assignment in Part 2. Here you are able to consolidate your skills as you work through the exercises. At this stage the emphasis is on dealing with information (in hard copy and electronic format) and on following and carrying out instructions accurately to produce the required results. There are further hints and tips on achieving these goals.

Specimen answers to exercises are given at the end of the book. At this level, you have a considerable amount of freedom over layout, etc and so you may notice that the answers do not always look exactly like yours. However, you must check that all criteria have been met. Your tutor will be able to advise you.

The syllabus and assessment details are provided on page 160 and other useful information including changing default settings, file management, document layout and forms for completion while undertaking the assignments, etc is to be found in the appendix.

Scenario

You work for a company called Naturetrail Holidays. This organisation has properties for rent during the spring and summer months. The annual presentation to regional offices is about to take place.

The Publicity Officer will be doing the presentation and will need help in preparing materials that will be presented to regional office staff. You have been asked to help by extracting information stored in the database and spreadsheet files and to include this information in a publication and an automated presentation.

The publication will consist of a four-page leaflet (which will be used in conjunction with the annual brochure). The automated presentation will be on display in the foyer from the presentation day onwards.

You will need to access files from the accompanying disk in order to carry out some of the assignments. *So that you always have access to the original files, it is **essential** to make a copy of the disk before starting on any of the exercises.*

Note: During an actual assignment the scenario files are e-mailed to you. As you work through the exercises, you will need to note down details on a File Store Record Sheet. This can be found in the appendix.

 INFO

There are many ways of performing a task in Windows 98 and Office 2000 applications – for example, via the keyboard, using the mouse or using the menus. For simplicity, the practical exercises usually show one method. There are, however, instructions for other methods in the quick reference guides or in the appendix. You will then be able to decide which is the best method for you.

Note: In this book the terms **click on**, **select** and **press** are used to distinguish between mouse, menu and keyboard actions. For example:

Click on: the **Save** button
From the **File** menu, select: **Save**
Press: **Ctrl + S**

Getting help

There are quick reference guides at the end of chapters and useful information in the appendix. In addition, in all Office 2000 applications there is a **Help** menu, or pressing **F1** will activate the application's **Help** dialogue box. There is also the Office Assistant. Throughout the book, I have hidden this facility so as not to be distracted from the main objectives. More details on the Office Assistant can be found in the appendix.

PART *1*

Explanation and exercises

Chapter 1

Electronic communications using Outlook Express

1 Getting started

In this section you will learn how to:
- understand electronic mail (e-mail) basics
- load Outlook Express
- understand the Outlook Express window
- create messages
- transmit messages
- route/address messages
- exit Outlook Express.

1.1 Understanding electronic mail (e-mail) basics

Electronic mail (e-mail) is a method of sending information from one computer to another. You can send and receive the electronic equivalent of letters, faxes, pictures and sound. Some organisations have their own internal e-mail systems for communications between colleagues. Others are connected to the Internet in order to send and receive e-mail locally and internationally. It is a quick and efficient means of communication. It has the advantage that you can send and receive your messages when you choose (unlike telephone communication). Due to its flexibility and cost effectiveness, it is being adopted at an ever-increasing rate.

This chapter focuses on sending and receiving e-mail using Microsoft Outlook Express 5. In demonstrating the methods used by Outlook Express you will gain an insight into the procedures involved even though you may be using a different e-mail system. It should be relatively easy to apply what you learn here to your own e-mail system.

Note: Since Outlook Express can be configured to suit your needs, the Outlook Express settings used in this chapter may differ slightly from your settings. This could result in some of the methods given not conforming exactly to those you may see on your computer.

1.2 Loading Outlook Express

Exercise 1 Load Outlook Express.

METHOD I 1 In the Windows 98 desktop, click on: the **Start** button – a menu appears.
2 Select **Programs** by moving the mouse over it – another menu appears.
Click on: **Outlook Express** (Figure 1.1).

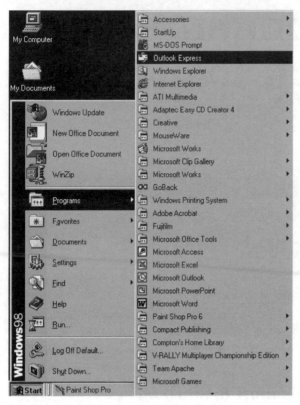

Figure 1.1 Loading Outlook Express from the Start menu

METHOD 2 (*Use this method if you have a shortcut icon to Outlook Express on your desktop.*)
1 In the Windows 98 desktop on the taskbar, click on: the **Launch Outlook Express** shortcut icon:

Either method will result in the Outlook Express window being displayed on screen (Figure 1.2).

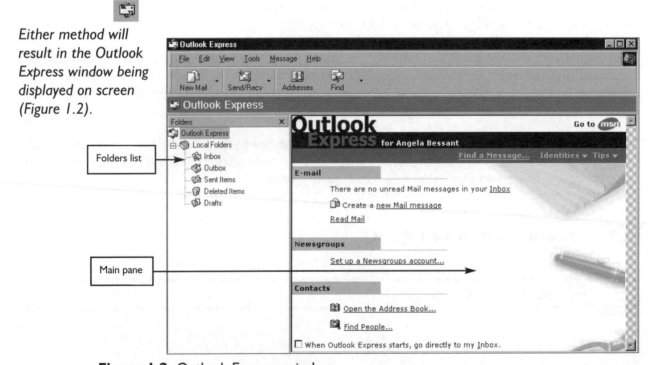

Figure 1.2 Outlook Express window

The Folders list contains:

- Inbox folder – where incoming messages are stored
- Outbox folder – where outgoing messages are stored
- Sent Items folder – where sent messages are stored
- Deleted Items folder – where deleted messages are stored
- Drafts folder – where draft messages are stored.

The main pane displays updates about your mail and shortcuts for commonly used activities.

1.3 Creating messages

Exercise 2 Create the message shown below and send it to someone you know who has an e-mail address.

> *Note*: If you do not have anyone to send it to, then send it to your own e-mail address.
>
> Hi there [insert person's name]
>
> I am learning how to use e-mail. Please let me know if you have received this message.
>
> Thanks.
>
> [Insert your name.]

METHOD 1 Click on: the **New Message** button (see Figure 1.2):

Note: The text on the button is New Mail.

The New Message window appears (Figure 1.3).

2 Click in the **To:** box and enter the e-mail address of the person you are sending the message to. Check that you have keyed in the address correctly.

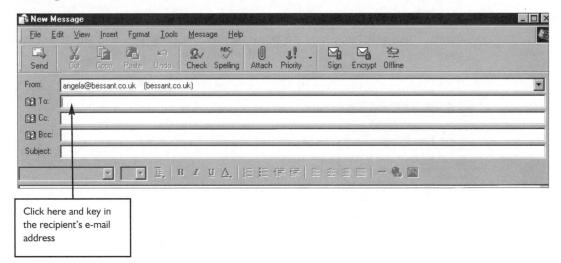

Click here and key in the recipient's e-mail address

Figure 1.3 New Message window

INFO

It is very important that the address is keyed in correctly otherwise it will not reach its destination. Each full stop is important. If you have made an error, you can delete it and key it in again.

E-mail addresses are made up of:

■ the user's name
■ followed by the @ symbol
■ followed by the address of the user's service provider.

For example:

J.Jones@somewhere.co.uk

3 Click in the subject line, and key in: **Just testing**.
4 Click in the space underneath and key in the message, as shown in Figure 1.4.

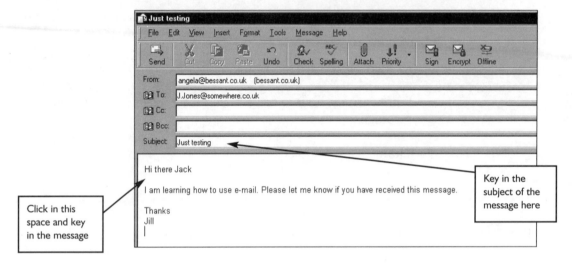

Figure 1.4 Creating a message

Note: The subject of your message **Just testing** has replaced **New Message** on the Title bar.

5 Click on: the **Send** button

Note: The spellcheck may be activated automatically at this stage (depending on your settings).

6 The Dial-up Connection dialogue box may appear (Figure 1.5).

Figure 1.5 Dial-up Connection

7 Click on: **Work Offline**

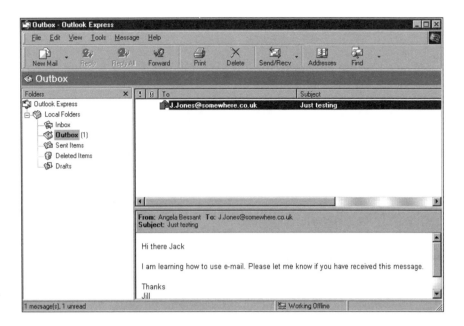

Figure 1.6 Message stored in Outbox folder waiting to be transmitted

8 You are returned to the Outlook Express window (Figure 1.6). You can see that your Outbox now has a (1) next to it and the message is in the right pane:

INFO

You have composed your message 'offline' – ie not connected to the phone line and therefore not incurring phone costs. When you have learnt how to use e-mail, it is a good idea to compose several messages and then send them all at the same time since there is a minimum phone call charge. They will be stored in your Outbox folder until you are ready to send them but in this example we are sending just one message. Outlook Express will automatically check if there are any incoming messages at the same time as sending messages.

1.4 *Transmitting messages*

Exercise 3 Transmit the message you have prepared.

METHOD **1** Click on: the **Send and Receive All** button:

2 Outlook Express will ask if you want to go online now. Click on: **Yes**.
3 The Dial-up Connection dialogue box is displayed (Figure 1.5). Click on: **Connect**.
4 The message will be sent automatically.
5 When it has been transmitted, it is placed in the **Sent Items** folder. Click on: the folder to check.

INFO

Outlook Express can be set up to connect/disconnect automatically from the phone line. If this is not set you will need to do this manually and you should be prompted to do so. When you are connected to the phone line, the following icon will be visible on the Taskbar:

Right-click on this icon for a menu with the option to disconnect.

1.5 Routing/addressing messages

The same message can be sent to more than one address at a time.

Exercise 4 Compose the following message and send it to two different e-mail addresses:

> Just to remind you that due to the weather the annual barbecue has been postponed and will now take place next Wednesday. Please e-mail me to confirm that you can still come.
>
> Thanks
>
>
> [Your name]

There are several ways to send the same message to more than one person. Two methods are shown below. Method 1 sends the messages on equal terms to both recipients. In Method 2 the main recipient is the person in the **To**: box, with a 'carbon copy' sent to the second addressee. Use this method only if you are asked to 'cc' the message to the second recipient.

METHOD I   I   In the **To**: box, key in in the e-mail addresses and separate them with semi-colons. For example:
  J.Jones@somewhere.co.uk;A.Smith@somewhereelse.co.uk

  Note: You don't need a space after the semi-colon.

METHOD 2   I   In the **To**: box, key in the first person's e-mail address.
  2   In the **Cc**: box, key in the second person's e-mail address.

  Create the message (as in Section 1.3) and transmit the message (as in Section 1.4) to the two addresses.

  Note: The message is again placed in your **Sent** folder and is still treated as one message, even though it has been transmitted to two different addresses.

1.6 Exiting Outlook Express

Exercise 5 Exit Outlook Express.

METHOD   From the **File** menu, select: **Exit**.

2 Receiving and printing attachments

In this section you will learn how to:

■ access received messages, forward messages and reply to sender
■ print messages including records of transactions
■ attach files to messages
■ view attached files.

2.1   Accessing received messages

Exercise 1   Access messages received.

Note: If you have not yet received a reply to your e-mails then you will need to send an e-mail to your own e-mail address as a demonstration, so that you have a received message.

METHOD   1 Load Outlook Express as in Section 1.2 (if not already loaded).
2 You will notice that there is a number next to your Inbox folder (Figure 1.7).

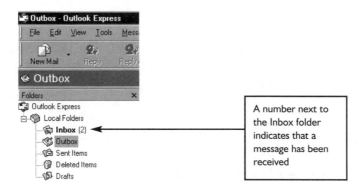

A number next to the Inbox folder indicates that a message has been received

Figure 1.7   Inbox folder

3 Click on: **Inbox**. The message(s) will be displayed in the right-hand pane.
4 Click once on the message to see it in the Preview pane – bottom right – (Figure 1.8), or double-click on it to see it in a separate window.

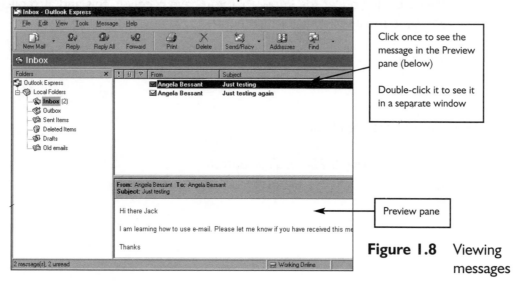

Click once to see the message in the Preview pane (below)

Double-click it to see it in a separate window

Preview pane

Figure 1.8   Viewing messages

2.2 *Printing messages including records of transactions*

Sometimes you may want to print an e-mail message (this is a requirement for IBT III).

Exercise 2 Print a copy of a message you have received.

METHOD
1 Ensure the message is visible in its own window (see Section 2.1.4 above).
2 From the **File** menu, select: **Print**; the Print dialogue box appears.
3 Check that the printer is ready and loaded with paper.
4 Click on: **OK**.

i **INFO**

You will notice that your printed copy includes transaction details. This is required for IBT III.

2.3 *Attaching files to messages*

Sometimes you may want to enclose something with your message, eg a picture or a different type of file. In such cases you can add a file to your message. This is called an attachment. You can add more than one file. These are then called attachments.

Exercise 3 Create a simple Excel or Word file. Save the file with the filename **TEST**. Send a message, together with the file **TEST** (the attachment), to an e-mail address. Ask the recipient to send you an attachment back.

METHOD
1 Create a simple file and save it with the name **TEST** in a place where you will know where to find it (eg on a floppy disk in drive A).
2 Load Outlook Express and key in the following message:

Hi [name of recipient]

I am practising sending and receiving attachments to e-mail messages. Please find the attached file TEST.

Please could you let me know that you have received this and also please could you send me an example attachment?

Thanks.

[Your name]

Note: Do not click send yet.

3 Click on: the **Attach File** toolbar button:

4 The Insert Attachment dialogue box appears.
5 Select the drive where the file is located, eg Drive A.
Click on: the file so that it appears in the **File name:** box (or key in the filename).
6 Click on: **Attach** (Figure 1.9).

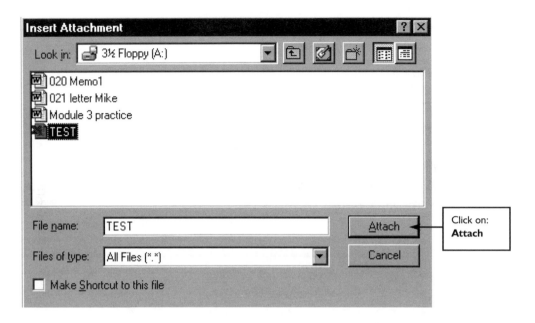

Figure 1.9 Insert Attachment dialogue box

7 You will notice that your attachment is now shown in the **Attach** box that has appeared (Figure 1.10).

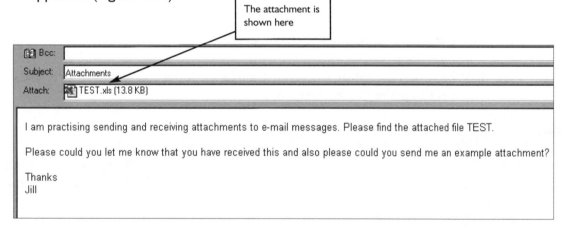

Figure 1.10 E-mail with attachment

8 You can now send the file in the normal way.

i __INFO__

You can attach more than one file to a message by repeating steps 3–6 for each extra file.

2.4 *Viewing attachments*

Exercise 4 View an attachment you have received.

METHOD

When you receive a message with an attachment, the message has a paperclip icon next to it, as shown in Figure 1.11.

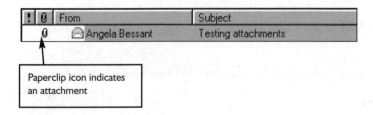

Figure 1.11 Attachment received icon

1 Double-click on: the message to view it in a separate window.
2 Double-click on: the attached file (Figure 1.12). The file will appear in its own program window.

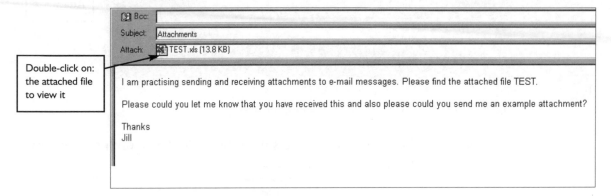

Figure 1.12 Opening an attachment

3 When you have finished viewing the file, close its window in the normal way. You are returned to Outlook Express.

 INFO

When you have received messages you can use the **Reply to Sender** button to send a message back. This automatically enters the e-mail address and subject in the relevant boxes. Click in the message area and key in your reply. You can delete the original messages, if you want to, by selecting the text to delete and pressing **Delete**. Use the **Forward** button to send the message on to another e-mail address. You can enter your own message (as above) along with the one you are forwarding if you want to. Transmit in the normal way.

In Chapter 2 you will learn how to save e-mail attachments before viewing them. This can safeguard against the spread of computer viruses.

2.5 **Exit**

Exit Outlook Express as shown in Section 1.6.

Outlook Express quick reference for IBT III

Action	Keyboard	Mouse	Right-mouse menu	Menu
Access received messages		Click: **Inbox** in left-hand pane Click: the message (to view in Preview) *or* Double-click: the message (to view in own window)		
Attach files to messages		Click: the 📎 **Attach File** button		**Insert, File Attachment**
Create messages		Click: the 🗋 New Mail **New Message** button		
Exit Outlook Express		Click: the ☒ **Close** button		**File, Exit**
Foward message		Click: the Forward **Forward** button		
Load Outlook Express	In Windows 98 desktop			
		Click: the 🖫 **Launch Outlook Express** shortcut icon		**Start, Programs, Outlook Express**
Print messages (including those with attachments)	(With transaction details and message visible in its own window)			
	Ctrl + P	Click: the 🖨 **Print** button		**File, Print**
Reply to Sender		Click: the Reply **Reply to Sender** button		
Route/address messages *Multiple recipients*	Key in the address in the **To**: box Separate addresses with semicolons (;) Use **Cc** box to send a 'carbon copy'			
Transmit messages	**Ctrl + Enter**	Click: the **Send and Receive All** button 📧 Send/Recv		**Tools, Send and Receive All**
View attachments	(With message in its own window – attachment visible)			
		Double-click: the attachment		

Hints and tips

Common errors made when completing IBT III assignments:

- Double-check that you have keyed in the *exact* e-mail address.
- Have you attached the correct file(s), and only the correct file(s), to the e-mail message?
- Have you printed out a message and transaction details when requested?
- Ensure you have disconnected after sending/receiving messages.

There are many more features to Outlook Express which are beyond the scope of this book. Experiment with the menus and toolbar buttons. Use the online Help to find out more about topics you are particularly interested in.

Chapter 2

File management using Windows Explorer

1 Getting started

In this section you will learn how to:

- start Explorer
- create directories/folders
- create subdirectories/subfolders
- manage files
  - save/name
  - retrieve
  - copy/move
  - delete
- record file storage details
- exit Explorer.

This chapter concentrates on Windows Explorer 98 to demonstrate file management, although some file management can be carried out within programs like Word and Excel (see the appendix).

Note: Much of this chapter was covered for the IBT II qualification, but is repeated here for revision purposes.

Windows Explorer allows you to view all the folders and files on your computer. It can be used for disk and file management.

 INFO

Windows 98 uses the word 'folder' and not 'directory'. Some older versions of Windows refer to folders as directories.

When carrying out the following exercises, if you suspect things have gone wrong, pressing the **Esc** key will usually cancel a command in progress.

1.1 *Starting Explorer*

From the **Start** menu, select: **Programs**, then **Windows Explorer**. The Explorer window appears. Figure 2.1 shows the $3\frac{1}{2}$ Floppy (A:) drive selected in the left pane; the contents of the disk in drive A are displayed in the pane on the right.

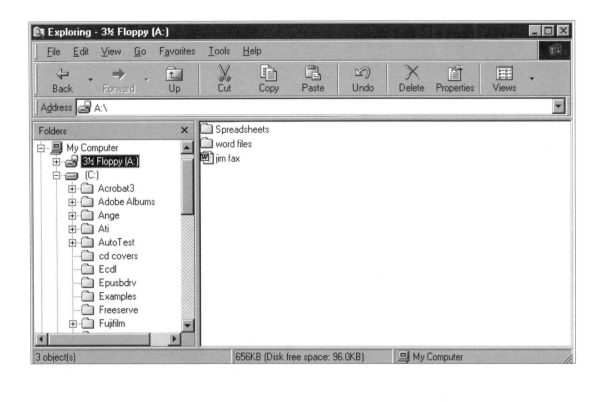

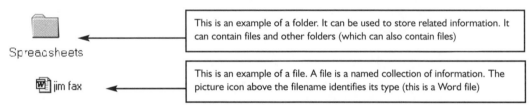

Figure 2.1   Folders and files

Displaying the contents of a folder

Double-click on: the folder.

> **INFO**
>
> It is better to double-click on the icon rather than the text as, sometimes, you will not get the action you expect (if you have not double-clicked properly). Instead a box may appear around the text, waiting for your input. If this happens, press the **Esc** key and try again.

1.2   *Creating a new folder*

> **INFO**
>
> You can create new folders in which to store related documents. This is always good practice as it makes for easier location of files. Always give folders and files meaningful names that you will be able to remember at a later date.

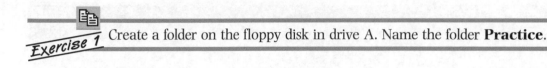

Exercise 1 Create a folder on the floppy disk in drive A. Name the folder **Practice**.

METHOD 1 With a disk in drive A, in the left-hand (Folders) pane, click on: **3½ Floppy (A:)**.
2 The contents of the floppy disk in drive A are displayed in the right-hand pane.
3 Right-click in the white space of this pane: a menu appears (Figure 2.2).

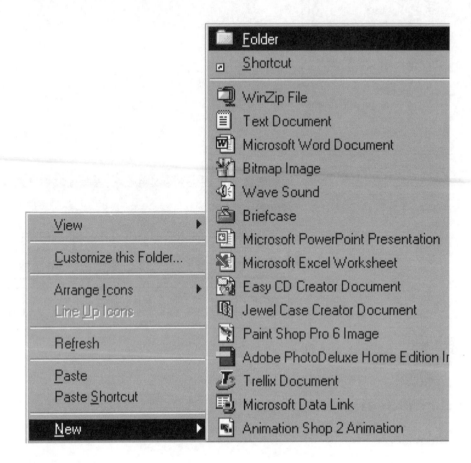

Figure 2.2 Creating a new folder

4 Select: **New** and then **Folder**.
5 Key in a name, **Practice** for the new folder and press **Enter** (Figure 2.3).

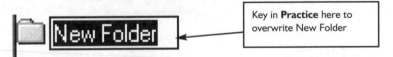

Key in **Practice** here to overwrite New Folder

Figure 2.3 New folder

1.3 *Creating a subfolder*

A subfolder is a folder within a folder.

Exercise 2 Create a subfolder named **wp** within the folder **Practice**.

METHOD I In the **Folders** pane, double-click on: **3½ Floppy (A:)**. The folder **Practice** is listed. Click on: the **Practice** folder to select it. It opens and **Exploring – Practice** is displayed on the Title bar (Figure 2.4).

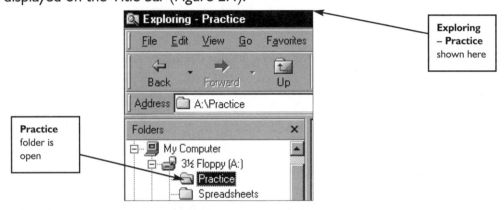

Figure 2.4 Exploring – Practice

2 From the **File** menu, select: **New** and then **Folder** (Figure 2.5).

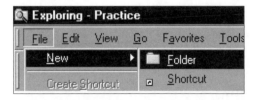

Figure 2.5 New Folder

3 A new folder appears in the right-hand pane and you will notice that a + sign has appeared next to the folder **Practice** in the left-hand pane. This denotes that the folder **Practice** has a subfolder.
Key in a name, **wp** for the folder. Press: **Enter** (Figure 2.6).

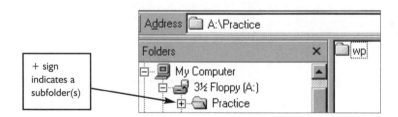

Figure 2.6 Creating a subfolder

Note: If you double-click on the folder **Practice** in the **Folders** pane, the subfolder **wp** will be displayed:

You can create numerous subfolders within a folder, following the method above. You can also create subfolders within subfolders if you wish.

1.4 Deleting a folder/file

1 Select the folder/file you want to delete by clicking it. Press: **Delete**. You will be asked to confirm the delete.
2 Click on: **Yes**.

Note: When you delete a folder, its contents are also deleted including all subfolders and files.

The Recycle Bin

You can restore a deleted file (**not one deleted from a floppy disk**) from the Recycle Bin by clicking on the **Recycle Bin** icon on the Windows desktop, selecting the file you want to restore and selecting **Restore** from the **File** menu.

Emptying the Recycle Bin

It is a good idea to remove files from the Recycle Bin from time to time. To do this:

1 Click on: the **Recycle Bin** to select it.
2 From the **File** menu, select: **Empty Recycle Bin**.

1.5 Saving and naming files

Files are normally saved and named within their applications, eg word processing files are saved and named when using Word.

1.6 Copying files

Exercise 3 Create a short file in Word. Save the file with the name **Short File** on a floppy disk in drive A. Copy this file to the folder **Practice**, which you created earlier.

METHOD 1 Create and save the Word file on the A drive. Close the Word file.
2 Start Explorer and select: **Floppy (A:)** if it is not already selected. The file you have saved is displayed in the right pane (Figure 2.7).

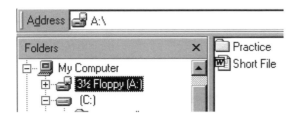

Figure 2.7 Contents window displaying file

3 There are three main ways to copy the file:

METHOD 1   Select the file **Short File**, hold down the left mouse button and, at the same time, hold down the **Ctrl** key. Drag the file to the folder **Practice**. Release the **Ctrl** key and the mouse button.

METHOD 2   **a** Select the file **Short File**, hold down the right mouse button and drag the file to the folder **Practice**.
   b Release the mouse button – a menu appears.
   c Select: **Copy Here**.

METHOD 3   **a** Right-click on: the file **Short File** – a menu appears:

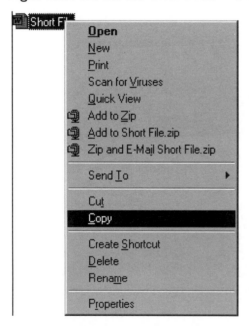

   b Select: **Copy**.
   c Right-click where you want to copy to.
   d Select: **Paste**.

 INFO

The third method is sometimes easier when you have numerous files and folders, as they may scroll out of view when you try to drag them.

You can check that the file is in the **Practice** folder by clicking on it to reveal its contents.

Note: Folders can be copied in the same way.

1.7 *Moving files*

Files/folders can be moved following the methods above, except:

METHOD 1 Do not hold down the **Ctrl** key when moving files/folders.

METHOD 2 At stage **c** select: **Move here**.

METHOD 3 At stage **b** select: **Cut**. At stage **c** right-click where you want to move to.

Selecting multiple files

You can select more than one file to delete, copy or move.

Selecting a group of files:

1 Select the first file in the group.
2 Hold down the **Shift** key on the keyboard and select the last file you want.

Selecting any files (not grouped together):

1 Select the first file.
2 Hold down the **Ctrl** key on the keyboard and select each file in the group.

1.8 *Recording file storage details*

For the IBT III assessment you will be asked to record file storage details on a File Store Record Sheet so that tutors can confirm they are able to recall your work. For the purposes of this book, there is a practice File Store Record Sheet in the appendix. (*Note*: This is not exactly the same as the OCR/RSA document.)

Ensure you have entered all the details requested:

■   Your name.
■   The name of the directory (folder) for the IBT III project.
■   Step number, subdirectory (subfolder), filename or reference, query/report name.
■   Also ensure you have ticked the end box if the file is to be used later in the assignment.

Note: Practise using a File Record Sheet throughout the Naturetrail Holidays scenario exercises.

1.9 *Exiting Explorer*

From the **File** menu, select: **Close**.

2 Copying attachments

In this section you will learn how to:
■   copy attachments to folders and subfolders.

2.1   Copying attachments to folders and subfolders

Exercise 1   Copy an e-mailed attachment to a folder.

METHOD   **I**   Load Outlook Express in order to access your mailbox.

If you do not have a received message with an attachment, then send one to your own e-mail address. Also ensure you have a folder where you can store the attachment. For the purposes of this exercise, use the **TEST** file, created in Chapter I, Section 2.3, and put it into the folder **Practice** also created earlier in Chapter 2, Section I.2.

2   Double-click on the message so that it appears in its own window (Figure 2.8).

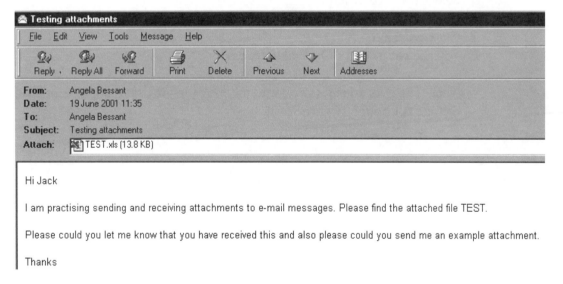

Figure 2.8 Testing attachments window

3   From the **File** menu, select: **Save Attachments** (Figure 2.9).

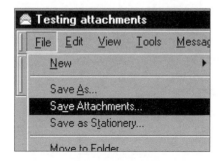

Figure 2.9 Saving attachment

4 The Save Attachments dialogue box appears (Figure 2.10).

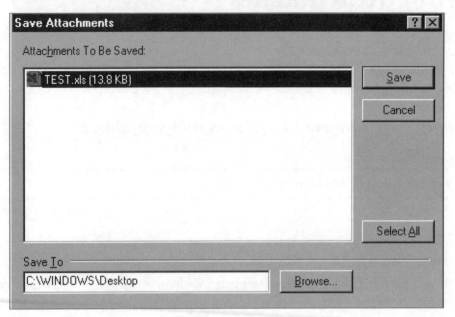

Figure 2.10 Save Attachments dialogue box

5 Select the attachment.
6 Click on: **Browse** and select the folder where you want to save the attachment.
7 Click on: **Save**.
8 You are returned to Outlook Express.

Note: The procedure is the same for multiple attachments, except that there is a **Select All** option (Figure 2.10).

File management quick reference for IBT III

Action	Keyboard	Mouse	Right-mouse menu	Menu
Copy e-mail attachments	With Outlook Express loaded and message in its own window			
			Save **As** or **Save All**	**File**, **Save Attac**h**ments**
Copy file/folder	Select the file/folder			
	Ctrl + C	Click: the 🖹 **Copy** button	**Copy**	**Edit**, **Copy**
	Click where you want to copy the file/folder			
	Ctrl + V	Click: the 🖹 **Paste** button	**Paste**	**Edit**, **Paste**
Create a new folder	Select where you want the new folder to be			
			New, **Folder**	**File**, **New**, **Folder**
Create a subfolder	Select the folder in which you want the subfolder to be and follow the steps for creating a new folder.			
Delete a file/folder	Select the file/folder			
	Delete		**Delete**	**File**, **Delete**
Display contents of folder		Double-click: the folder		
Exit Explorer		Click: the ⊠ **Close** button		**File**, **Close**
Load Explorer	In Windows 98 desktop			
				Start, **Programs**, **Windows Explorer**
Restore files	Double-click on: the **Recycle Bin** Select the file you want to restore			
			Right-click Select: **Restore**	**File, Restore**
Select files *files grouped together*	Click: the first file Holding down: **Shift**, click: the last file			
any files	Click: the first file Holding down: **Ctrl**, click: each file in turn			

Hints and tips
- For easier location, always give your files and folders/subfolders meaningful names.
- Use the File Store Record Sheet when requested to record details.
- Sometimes files are embedded in other files, eg charts in spreadsheet files, queries in database files. Ensure you note down where any embedded files are stored.

Practice exercise

This exercise is to help you practise the skills learnt in Chapter 2. Throughout the rest of this part of the book, you will be working through exercises and saving files in folders and subfolders.

Please create folders and subfolders for storage and retrieval of files as follows:

1 Create a folder to store your work in.

2 Record the folder name on your File Store Record Sheet.

3 Within this folder create and name two subfolders:

  ■ one is for working copies
  ■ one is for backup copies.

4 Record the names on your File Store Record Sheet.

Note: Use these folders and subfolders when saving files throughout Part 1 of this book. Record file details on the File Store Record Sheet.

Chapter 3

Databases using Access

1 Getting started

In this section you will revise and learn how to:
- access existing database files
- process existing database files
- insert data
  - records
  - fields
- edit data
  - text
  - numeric
- delete data
  - records
  - fields
- find and replace data
- format data.

i — **INFO**

If you have achieved competence at IBT Stage II, you will already be familiar with most of the database procedures above.

You will see (from the example Full Practice Assignment in Part 2) that at IBT Stage III you are given various tasks to perform with different delivery methods for the tasks, eg memos, data request forms. In this regard the assignments are meant to resemble actual office procedures. Therefore the skills required are analysis of the task, and selection and processing of the relevant data. Some of the tasks are appropriate for, and require action for, *both* the database and the spreadsheet assignments.

Spreadsheet skills are covered in the next chapter. In this chapter we will concentrate only on database skills. You are not expected to create a database file, but you will notice that the database files at this level are considerably larger than at IBT II level.

In order to aid understanding of these skills, the tasks are broken down in these chapters. You will be able to consolidate these skills by completing tasks in the context of the example Full Practice Assignment in Part 2. Detailed instructions for skills that were covered for IBT II are not given here. However, the quick reference guide at the end of this chapter should help you to remember any topics you may have forgotten.

Important

Before starting on the exercises, ensure you make a backup copy of the database files so that you have an original file to use with the example Full Practice Assignment given in Part 2.

1.1 *Accessing the appropriate file and adding a record*

 Exercise 1 — Load the appropriate database file and add the following property to it. Ensure you follow the existing upper- and lower-case conventions.

PROPERTY NAME	HEADLANDS
CODE	R691
LOCATION	RIVERS
OCCUPANTS	4
BEDROOMS	2
PARKING	YES
BOOKED(A)	7
BOOKED(B)	12
PRICE CODE	B
CHANGE DAY	SAT
DATE BOOKED	18 SEP 1999
AGENT	PAUL

METHOD   **1** Load the database file and the appropriate table.

i — **INFO**

The database filename is not given. When carrying out the IBT III assessment, there will be a choice of database files. They may look quite similar. Ensure you are working with the correct one by looking at the database in Table View and Table Design View, and matching the fields with the record to add to the database. If the fields are not the same or are not all there, you most likely are not working with the correct database file. Examine the other database files to see which one *exactly* matches the new record.

2 To insert a new record in a large database, use one of the following methods:
  a From the **Insert** menu, select: **New Record** and enter the record in the normal way.
  b Click on: the **New Record** ▶* button and enter the record in the normal way.
  c Go directly to the last record by clicking on: the ▶* button at the bottom of the table window.

Note: For each of the methods above, the cursor automatically moves to locate itself after the last record.

i __INFO__

Using the navigation buttons will help you to move quickly around the database file:

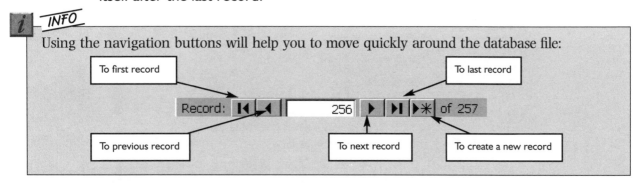

3 Follow any conventions that have already been set, eg upper case for text.
4 When you close, the changes are saved automatically and the records will be placed in the existing sort order.

1.2 *Deleting a record*

Exercise 2 Delete the following record:

PROPERTY NAME	GREEN
CODE	F642
LOCATION	FOREST

i __INFO__

With a large database file it is not sensible to scroll through all the records to find the one you are looking for. Instead use the following method.

METHOD 1 With the table displayed, position the cursor in the field you want to search – in this case we have been given details that are unique to this record ie PROPERTY NAME or CODE. In this example choose **PROPERTY NAME**:

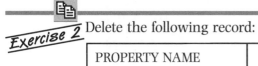

2 Click on: the 🔍 **Find** button.

3 The **Find and Replace** dialogue box appears. In the **Find What** box, key in the word **GREEN**. You will note that there are several options you may want to explore. Click on: **Find Next** (Figure 3.1).

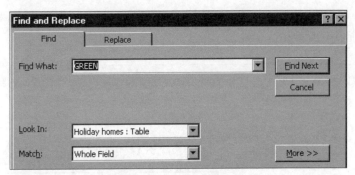

Figure 3.1 Find and Replace dialogue box

4 The PROPERTY NAME **GREEN** has been highlighted. Click on: **Cancel** (Figure 3.2).

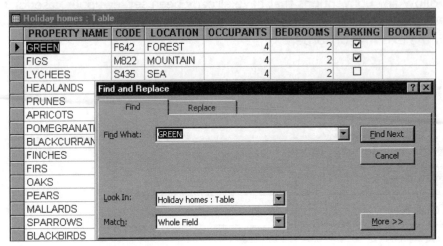

Figure 3.2 Find – **GREEN**

5 Delete the record in the normal way.

1.3 Deleting a field

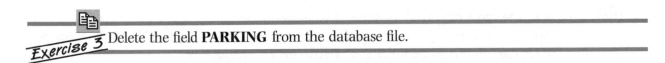

Exercise 3 Delete the field **PARKING** from the database file.

1 In Table Design View, select the field to be deleted by clicking to the left of it as shown. The entire field is highlighted (Figure 3.3).

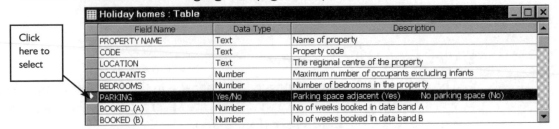

Figure 3.3 PARKING field

2 Press: **Delete**. A box appears. Click on: **Yes** (Figure 3.4).

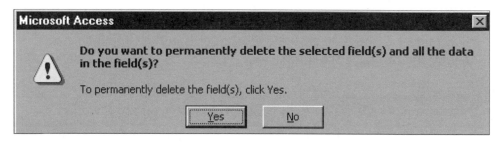

Figure 3.4 Deleting a field

3 Close Table Design View. You are prompted to save changes. Click on: **Yes**.

1.4 Adding a field

Exercise 4 It has been decided to add TVs to all COUNTRY properties. Add a new field **TV** to the database file. This field will show those properties that have a TV and those that do not. Set up the field accordingly between the PRICE CODE field and the CHANGE DAY field.

METHOD

1 In Table Design View, position the cursor in the field below where the new field is to be, ie in the CHANGE DAY field.
2 Right-click – a menu appears.
3 Select: **Insert Rows**. A new row appears above the CHANGE DAY field (Figure 3.5).
4 Enter the details for the new field in the normal way. *Hint:* The Data Type will be Yes/No.
5 Save changes.
6 In Table (Datasheet) View, click in the boxes in the TV field to add TV to the records of COUNTRY properties only. *Hint:* Change the sort order to LOCATION so all the records to amend are grouped together.

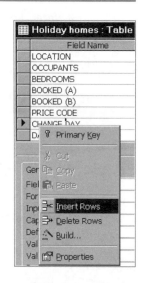

Figure 3.5 Insert Rows

1.5 Editing data

Exercise 5 It has been noticed that one of the properties has been entered incorrectly. Please amend as follows:

	ENTERED AS	SHOULD READ
CODE	M342	M340
BOOKED(A)	8	7
BOOKED(B)	14	10

METHOD I Find the record by clicking on: the **Find** button and following the method shown in Section 1.2, this time ensuring the cursor is in the CODE field.
2 Edit the record in the normal way.

Exercise 6 Please amend all properties BOOKED(A) from 6 weeks to 7 weeks.

 INFO

This time you will be looking for multiple entries since there is likely to be more than one.

METHOD I Move the cursor to the top of the database file (**Ctrl + Home**).
2 Position the cursor in the BOOKED(A) field and then from the **Edit** menu, select: **Replace**. The Find and Replace dialogue box is displayed.
3 Enter 6 in the **Find What** box and 7 in the **Replace With** box.
4 In the **Look In** box, click on: the down arrow and select: **BOOKED (A)**.
5 Click on: **Replace All**.
6 Close the Find and Replace dialogue box.

Note: There should be seven records to change.

 INFO

If you are replacing only parts of an entry eg all codes beginning M9 or 28, use the options in the **Match box**.

1.6 *Formatting data*

Ensure you have conformed to the formatting that is already on the database file (or, in an IBT III assignment, any instructions that you may be given) and that you do not have lower-case entries in those fields where upper case is already entered.

 INFO

You may find it helpful to print out the database file at this stage and check that you have correctly completed all the exercises in this section. The amended database file is used in the next section.

Ensure all fields fit to one page for easier reading and to save wasting paper. Do this by changing column widths (ensure that headings and contents are still fully visible) and using **Page Setup** to alter margins.

2 Creating queries and reports, printing and transferring data

In this section you will revise and learn how to:

- create and run queries containing up to five specified criteria
- print data as specified
- create reports and display data as specified
- transfer data between files/applications.

_i_ INFO

The following practice exercises are based on the amended (in the last section) database file. Answers to the exercises are given at the end of the book, including the designs for the queries. Please note that, at this level, some aspects of layout are at your discretion so your answer may not look exactly the same as the one given. However, you should check you have met all the criteria requested.

2.1   Creating, running and printing queries

Exercise 1 Load the database file, which was amended in the previous section, and create, run and print the following query:

QUERY

Fields/headings to print	All (in the existing order)
Sort order	Ascending order of CODE
Search criteria	BOOKED(A) 7 or less; PRICE CODE B; DATE BOOKED 18 September 1999 or later
Other details (please specify)	Field headings must be shown

Printout required   Yes ✓   No ☐   Fit one page ✓

METHOD   1   Carry out the query in the normal way. See the Working with Queries info box overleaf for guidance on designing your query. Save your query as **Query1**.

Working with queries

Queries can seem quite complicated at this level and may have as many as five specified criteria. Take each criterion in turn and remember to check (in Design View) that you have done everything you have been asked. In Datasheet View, check again that the results match up with what has been requested and that the search order is correct.

Use the following as a guide:

In the Criteria row you can enter any of the following:

❑ An exact match, eg SMITHSON

❑ The wildcard *

The * wildcard stands for any number and type of character, eg if you were unsure how to spell the name you could enter SM*THSON or SM*SON. You can place the * wildcard before, after and between characters and you can use it more than once in a single field, eg SM*TH*.

❑ The wildcard ?

The ? wildcard acts as a placeholder for one character, eg SM?THSON.

❑ LIKE

This tells Access not to look for an exact match, eg LIKE SMYTHSON.

❑ NOT

If you want to find all the records but not SMITHSON you could enter NOT SMITHSON.

❑ NULL

If you have records with no value in the field, you can type NULL to find these records, eg if you were looking for all properties without central heating and the database design had allowed no value in the central heating field for properties without central heating but a YES value for those with central heating.

❑ Mathematical operators

>	more than	>=	more than or equal to
<	less than	<=	less than or equal to
=	equal to	<>	not equal to

❑ AND and OR

You can use AND when you need to restrict results, eg for all employees aged over 20 and under 30 use >20 AND <30. You can use OR when you want a combination of results: GREEN OR RED OR BLUE.

❑ Fields containing YES/NO data. If YES the data will show as a ticked box. Use YES if you want to find the ticked box data and NO if not.

❑ Working with dates:

Before 12 September 1999	<12 September 1999 (note: You can use an abbreviated version of the date and it will change to the correct format, eg 12/9/99)
After 12 September 1999	>12 September 1999
12 September 1999 or after	>=12 September 1999
12 September 1999 or before	<=12 September 1999
12 September 1999 to 18 September 1999 inclusive	>11 September 1999 and <19 September 1999

2 When printing the query, use Print Preview to ensure it fits on one page. If it does not fit, you can alter the following:

  a From the **File** menu, select: **Page Setup**:
   – with the **Margins** tab selected, you can alter the left and right margins
   – with the **Page** tab selected, you can set the printout to landscape.

  b If it still does not fit, you could reduce the width of the columns.
   (*Note*: Headings **must** be shown in full unless requested otherwise.)

  c You could **Select All** (**Ctrl + A**) and reduce the font size (use the **Format** menu, **Font**).

Exercise 2

Create, run and print out the following query:

QUERY

Fields/headings to print	PROPERTY NAME, LOCATION, BOOKED(A), PRICE CODE
Sort order	Descending order of PROPERTY NAME
Search criteria	PROPERTY NAME beginning with the letter S, the letter G or the letter M; LOCATION Sea or Forest; OCCUPANTS 4 or more; CHANGE DAY Saturday; BOOKED(B) more than 8 weeks
Other details (please specify)	Show only required fields in specified order, including field headings.

Printout required   Yes ✓   No ☐   Fit one page ✓

METHOD

  1 Carry out the query in the normal way.

   Notes:
   a You will need to use the wildcard for the PROPERTY NAME search.
   b You will need to widen the PROPERTY NAME column in Design View to accommodate all the criteria on the same row.
    Note: Do not enter criteria on a separate row.
   c Some of the fields in the search criteria should not be shown.
    Hint: It is a good idea to run the query with these fields showing so that you can check it has achieved the required results. Remember to switch back to Design View, to remove the ticks from the boxes in the Show row and to resave the query.

  2 Save the query as **Query 2**.
  3 Print the query in the normal way.

Exercise 3 Create, run and print out the following query:

QUERY

Fields/headings to print	PROPERTY NAME, LOCATION, BOOKED(A), CHANGE DAY, AGENT
Sort order	Ascending BOOKED(A)
Search criteria	Weeks BOOKED(A) 7 to 14 inclusive; Weeks BOOKED(B) 12 or more; AGENT Paul or Gail
Other details (please specify)	Show only required fields in specified order, including field headings.

Printout required   Yes ✓   No ☐   Fit one page ✓

INFO

Sometimes you may need to create a query that will require entries in the **Or** row in Query Design View eg LOCATION: SEA, PRICE CODE: B and LOCATION: RIVERS, PRICE CODE: D. In this instance the **Criteria** row would contain the SEA locations and the **Or** row the RIVERS locations so that the differing PRICE CODES can be entered in their separate rows,

METHOD
1. Create and run the query in the normal way.
2. Save this query as **Query3**.
3. Print the query.

2.2 *Creating reports and displaying data as specified*

Exercise 4 Create a report as specified below:

REPORT/EXTRACT

Report format   Group ☐   Column ✓   Tabular ☐

Title	LOW BOOKINGS PERIOD A
Fields/headings to print	PROPERTY NAME and BOOKED(A) only in this order
Sort order	PROPERTY NAME ascending
Other details (please specify)	Using Query1 (saved in Exercise 1) produce a report to be used where specified in the publication.

| Printout required | Yes ✓ | No ☐ | To be dated | Yes ☐ | No ✓ |
| Fit one page | Yes ✓ | No ☐ | Page numbered | Yes ☐ | No ✓ |

Important!   This report will be used in the publication assignment in Chapter 6.

METHOD   Create the report using the **Report Wizard**.

Notes:
a When working through the Report Wizard, remember to base the report on
Query1 (Figure 3.6).

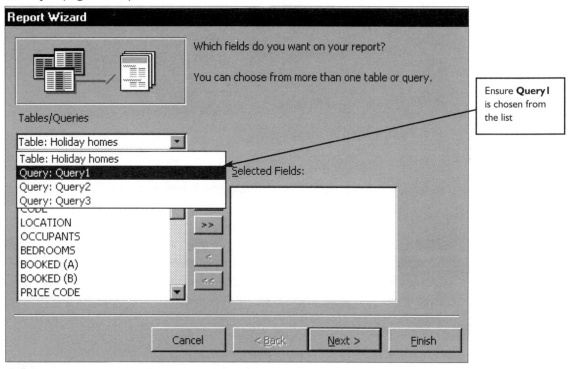

Figure 3.6 Report Wizard – selecting Query1

b Ensure **Columnar** is chosen at the stage shown in Figure 3.7.

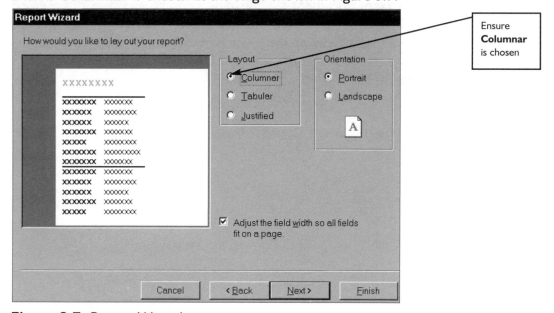

Figure 3.7 Report Wizard

c When choosing the style for the report, **Compact** works best as it requires fewer changes in Design View to fit in all the entries in their entirety.

d The Report Preview should look similar to the one shown in Figure 3.8.

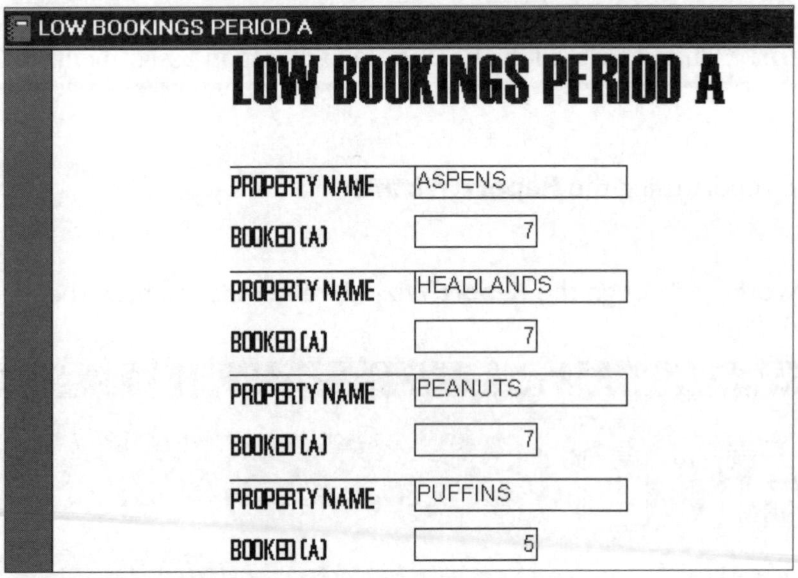

Figure 3.8 Report Preview

Note: If you scroll down you will notice that the report has the date and page number at the bottom. You have been asked not to include this. Change to Design View and delete these items.

This is sufficient as a printout for this task. All the details are displayed in full. Sometimes this is not the case and it is very time consuming to alter it in Report Design View. It is also difficult to manipulate at a later stage. Therefore, it is easier if the report is output and saved in Word where it can be formatted more easily. The instructions for this are given below.

To output an Access report to Word:
1 With the Report Preview displayed, from the **Tools** menu, select: **Office Links** and then **Publish It with MS Word**.
2 The report is automatically output to Word.
3 Save the Word document in your folder. Ensure you save it as a Word document. *Note:* The document will automatically save in RTF format. Change this to a Word document in the **Save as type** box in the **Save As** dialogue box.
It is now easy to change the font and font size.
4 Print the report.
5 Close Word.

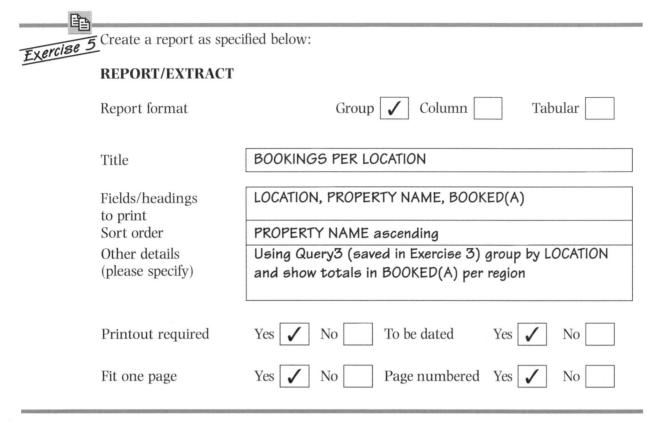

Exercise 5 Create a report as specified below:

REPORT/EXTRACT

Report format	Group ✓ Column ☐ Tabular ☐

Title	BOOKINGS PER LOCATION

Fields/headings to print	LOCATION, PROPERTY NAME, BOOKED(A)
Sort order	PROPERTY NAME ascending
Other details (please specify)	Using Query3 (saved in Exercise 3) group by LOCATION and show totals in BOOKED(A) per region

Printout required	Yes ✓ No ☐ To be dated Yes ✓ No ☐
Fit one page	Yes ✓ No ☐ Page numbered Yes ✓ No ☐

METHOD

1 Create the report using the **Report Wizard**, this time basing the report on **Query3**.

2 Select **LOCATION** when asked if you want to add any grouping levels as shown in Figure 3.9.

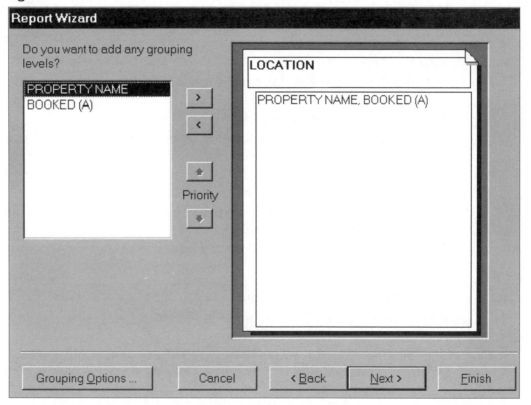

Figure 3.9 Grouping level Location

3 Experiment with different layouts at the stage in Figure 3.10. Stepped will work well for this report, as it leaves space to add the totals for BOOKED(A).

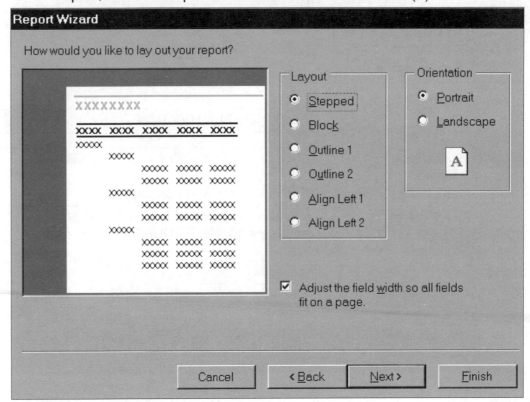

Figure 3.10 Report Wizard – Layout

4 The report is grouped by LOCATION as requested, but there are no totals per location in the BOOKED(A) column. The report can be output to Excel, where it can be manipulated with ease.

To output an Access report to Excel:
a With the Report Preview displayed, from the **Tools** menu, select: **Office Links** and then **Analyse It with MS Excel**.
b The report is automatically output to Excel.
c Here you can add any details you need, eg the totals BOOKED(A) per LOCATION, and format the spreadsheet as you like.
Note: You will notice that the report title has not been carried across. Insert a new row at the top of the spreadsheet and type in the report title.
d Add the other details requested, eg page number and date, to the spreadsheet (**View** menu, **Header and Footer**).
e Save the spreadsheet in your folder and print it.

---

i INFO

Report totalling can be carried out in Access. At step 3 of Report Wizard:
1 Click on: **Summary Options** to show totals as requested.
2 The Summary Options dialogue box is displayed.
3 Click in the **Sum** box so that a tick appears.
4 In the **Show** section, click in the **Detail and Summary** option button (to show all record detail).
5 Delete the summary text in Report Design View.

Access quick reference for IBT III

Action	Keyboard	Mouse	Right-mouse menu	Menu
Add a field	In Design View: Click in the field below where you want to insert a new field			
		Click: the ⧉ **Insert Rows** button	**Insert Rows**	**Insert**, **Rows**
	Add the field details Re-save the table design			
Add a record		Click: the ▶✳ **New Record** button OR Click: in the blank cell immediately after the last record	(Right-click to the left of any record) **New Record**	**Insert**, **New Record**
Change Data Type	(see separate table for Data Types) Click: in the **Data Type** box next to the field name you wish to change Click: the arrow Click: the Data Type you require eg Number Select the field properties (see separate table for Field Properties) from the box below Close the Table window, saving the table design			
Close a database	**Ctrl + W**	Click: the ☒ **Close** button on the database window		**File**, **Close**
Create a columnar report	Follow the method for creating a tabular report (see page 40) – except select **Columnar** instead of **Tabular**			
Create a database	Load Access Click: **Blank Access Database**, **OK** Select: the location Key in: the filename Click: **Create** Click: **Tables** tab. Double-click: **Create table in Design View**			
Create a query	In the Database window ensure the **Queries** tab is selected Double-click: **Create query in Design View** Click: **Add**, **Close**			
	The fields of the table are now displayed in a list box in the Query window. Place the fields that you want to see in your query in the field row of the query grid by double-clicking or dragging them. *Note:* Place the fields in the order that you want them to appear.			
Create a tabular report	Ensure the database is open and that the **Reports** tab is selected Double-click: **Create report by using wizard** Select: the name of the object – eg query, table – that the report is to be generated from Select the fields to include in the report using the 〉〉 or 〉 buttons Click: **Next** *(If you want to group the report – select the field(s) you want to group by here)* Click: **Next** *(If you want to change the sort order select the field you want to sort by and the sort order here)*			

Action	Keyboard	Mouse	Right-mouse menu	Menu
	Click: **Next** Select: **Tabular** Select the orientation you want – ie **Landscape** or **Portrait** Click: **Next** Select a style (Compact is good) Click: **Next**. Key in: the report title Click: **Finish**			
Delete a field	In Table Design View Select the field to be deleted by clicking to the left of it			
	Delete, **Y**	Click: the ⊟→ **Delete Rows** button Click: **Yes**	**Delete Rows**	**Edit**, **Delete Rows**
Delete a record	Select the record by clicking to the left of the first field of that record			
	Delete, **Y**	Click: the ⊠ **Delete Record** button Click: **Yes**	**Delete Record** **Yes**	**Edit**, **Delete Record**
	Select: **Yes** to save the change			
Edit data	Open the table (if it is not already open) Click: in the entry you want to edit Delete the old data Key in the new data			
Enter data	In the Database window Double-click the table to open it Enter the data required in the correct fields. Widen the field columns as necessary. Close the Table window. The data is saved automatically.			
Find a record	With the Table displayed, position the cursor in the field you want to search.			
	Ctrl + F	Click: the 🔍 **Find** button		**Edit**, **Find**
	In the Find What box, key in what you want to find Click: **Find Next** Continue until all records have been found *Note:* You may need to choose a field that has a unique entry to ensure you find the correct record.			
Load Access	In the Windows 98 desktop			
		Double-click: the **Microsoft Access** shortcut icon		**Start**, **Programs**, **Microsoft Access**
Open a table	In the Database window, make sure the **Tables** tab is selected			
in Datasheet View *in Design View*		Double-click: the table Click: the **View** button		

Action	Keyboard	Mouse	Right-mouse menu	Menu
Output a report	Ensure you are in the **Report Preview** view			
to Word or Excel		Click: the down arrow of **Office Links** button, select: **Analyze It with MS Excel** *OR* **Publish It with MS Word**		**Tools, Office Links, Publish it with MS Word** *OR* **Analyze it with MS Excel**
Print a query	In **Datasheet View**			
	Ctrl + P	Click: the 🖨 **Print** button		**File, Print**
Print a report	**Ctrl + P**	Click: the 🖨 **Print** button	**Print**	**File, Print**
Print, quick		Click: the 🖨 **Print** button Access will automatically print the whole table.		
Print specific fields	Use the **Show** row in the grid to choose whether or not to display a particular field in the query. A tick in the **Show** box means that the field will show, no tick means that it will not show. Click to toggle between them.			
Print a table	Open the table you want to print.			
	Ctrl + P			**File, Print**
	Make the necessary selections Choose Setup if you want to print Landscape Make the necessary selections from the Setup dialogue box Click: **OK, OK**			
Replace field entries	**Ctrl + H**			**Edit, Replace**
Save a query	**Ctrl + S**	Click: the 💾 **Save** button		**File, Save**
	To see the results of your query			
		Click: the ❗ **Run** button		**Query, Run**
Sort a query	Click: in the **Sort** box of the appropriate field Click: the ▾ arrow Select: **Ascending** or **Descending**.			
Sort records (quick sort)	Open the Table if it is not already open. Select the field that you want to sort by clicking on the Field Name at the top of the field column			
ascending order		Click: the ▲ᶻ↓ **Sort Ascending** button	**Sort Ascending**	
descending order		Click the ᶻ▾ **Sort Descending** button	**Sort Descending**	

Action	Keyboard	Mouse	Right-mouse menu	Menu
Specify criteria	Use the **Criteria** row in the grid to specify the conditions in a specific field – eg **RED** in the **Colour** field. (See *Working with Queries* page 32)			

Important: Always close the database file properly.

DATA TYPE	PROPERTIES
Text (the default)	No need to set, unless short of storage space.
Number	*Field Size* Long Integer is the default – this is OK for whole numbers. Double – for numbers with decimal places *Format* Choose **Fixed** for 2 decimal places to show (even if the last is a zero) Choose **Decimal Places** and enter the number required (Leave the Format blank for other numbers.)
Date/Time	Choose the most appropriate format for the task. (You can key in the date in any format and it will convert to the format you have set.)
Currency	Choose **Format Fixed** to display 2 decimal places with no commas or £ symbol.
Yes/No	No need to set

Hints and tips

■ At this level, you are not expected to create a database file. However, you will need to choose which database file to work with from those given. Examine the database files very carefully in order to establish which one is appropriate.

■ The files are quite large and it will not be immediately obvious, for example, if your query results are correct. It is therefore essential to carry out the work thoroughly in order to produce the required output.

■ Always check query criteria in Design View and remember to show only the requested fields in printouts.

■ Check that all the database-specified data is shown in full.

■ Proofread and double-check at all stages to ensure accuracy.

Chapter 4

Spreadsheets using Excel

1 Getting started

In this section you will revise and learn how to:
- access existing spreadsheet files
- process existing spreadsheet files
- insert data
  - columns
  - rows
- edit data
  - text
  - numeric
- delete data
  - columns
  - rows
- format data
  - case, borders, shading, font, character size.

Important

Before starting on the exercises below, ensure you make a backup copy of the spreadsheet file so you have an original file to use with the example Full Practice Assignment in Part 2.

1.1   *Accessing the appropriate file and inserting data*

Exercise 1 Load the appropriate spreadsheet file and add the following data to it (where it applies). Ensure you follow the existing upper- and lower-case conventions. Ensure the existing order of LOCATION is maintained and any necessary formulae replicated.

PROPERTY NAME	HEADLANDS
CODE	R691
LOCATION	RIVERS
OCCUPANTS	4
BEDROOMS	2
PARKING	YES
BOOKED(A)	7
BOOKED(B)	12
PRICE CODE	B
CHANGE DAY	SAT
DATE BOOKED	18 SEP 1999
AGENT	PAUL

METHOD   I Load the appropriate spreadsheet file.

INFO

It is important you take time to study the spreadsheet carefully. This will ensure you choose the appropriate one and enable you to work with it more effectively.

2 Enter *only* the relevant details into the spreadsheet following the instructions.

INFO

When asked to maintain the existing order, check carefully to see what that order is before inserting data. In this case, the sort order is ascending and, since the codes start with an alphabetic character, the numerical digits are taken in turn and not as their overall numeric value.

Exercise 2 All properties which have BOOKED(A) as 6 should be amended to 7.

METHOD   This is simply a matter of locating the appropriate cells and overwriting them.

Exercise 3 The entry for the Mountain property M342 has been entered incorrectly. Please amend it to M341. The BOOKED(A) column for this entry should read 7, not 8, and the BOOKED(B) column for this entry should read 13, not 14.

METHOD   Again, this is a matter of locating the appropriate cells and overwriting them.

Exercise 4 The Rivers property, property code R401, should not be entered on this spreadsheet. Please delete all reference to this property.

METHOD Delete the row containing this entry.

Exercise 5 1 Save the spreadsheet and record the details on the File Store Record Sheet.
2 Print the spreadsheet. Ensure it fits on one page.

Note: For the quickest way to ensure it fits on one page, use **Fit to Page** in **Page Setup**.

 INFO

The font type and size can be changed using the **Formatting** toolbar *or* the **Format** menu, **Cells**, **Font** tab, after selecting the cells to change or selecting all (**Ctrl + A**).

To add extra emphasis, cells can be given borders and shading. Use the **Format** menu, **Cells**, **Border** tab, after selecting the cell(s) to format. In the **Presets** section, click on the **Outline** button for an all-round border or in the **Border** section, click on the buttons for the border you require ie bottom, left etc. To shade cells, click on the **Patterns** tab, click on the colour required and then on **OK**.

2 Cell addresses, functions, replicating formulae, formatting data

In this section you will revise and learn:
- absolute cell addresses
- relative cell addresses
- named ranges/cells
- functions
    - sum
    - average
    - count
    - lookup
    - if

- how to replicate formulae
- how to format data
    - decimal places
    - integer
    - currency
    - alignment.

Omissions have been identified in the spreadsheet. Please check all sections and insert the relevant formulae and functions.

Use the following functions where appropriate:

SUM
AVERAGE
COUNT
LOOKUP

INFO

Excel can work out common tasks such as the ones above. These functions (and others) are built into Excel to make formulae easier and quicker to enter. You are already familiar with the SUM function. Other functions work in a similar way. The exact way of entering the formulae using functions is demonstrated as you work through the exercises.

Exercise 1 *Bookings section*
Calculate the total number of BOOKED(A) and BOOKED(B) for each of the six LOCATIONS. Display the figures as whole numbers without decimal places.

METHOD Check on the printout where these should appear. Use the **Autosum** button. Syntax is =SUM(cell ref:cell ref).

Note: You will not be able to replicate the formulae for the BOOKED(A) column but you will be able to replicate from BOOKED(A) to BOOKED(B) since you will already have the correct cell ranges.

Exercise 2 *Properties per location section*

Calculate the number of properties per location.

METHOD Use the COUNT function for this. Syntax is =COUNT(cell ref:cell ref).

1 Select the cell where the answer is to appear and key in =**COUNT(** (Figure 4.1).

PROPERTIES PER LOCATION	
LOCATION	NO OF PROPERTIES
COUNTRY	=COUNT(
FOREST	
LAKES	
MOUNTAIN	
RIVERS	
SEA	

Figure 4.1 Properties per location

2 Drag the mouse across the cells to count, ie the Country properties. A dotted line appears.

Note: The COUNT function will only work with numeric data, so we cannot use the PROPERTY CODE column – Figure 4.2.

	LOCATION AND PROPERTY CODE	BOOKED(A)	BO(
16			
17	COUNTRY		
18	C181	12	
19	C34	14	
20	C66	14	
21	C670	11	
22	C777	9	
23	C91	14	
24	C997	14	
25	FOREST		

Figure 4.2 Country properties

3 Press: **Enter**:

LOCATION	NO OF PROPERTIES
COUNTRY	=COUNT(B18:B24)

4 The result 7 appears in the cell.

5 Carry out the same process for each of the other locations.

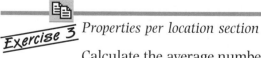

Exercise 3 *Properties per location section*

Calculate the average number of properties per location. Display the result as a whole number with no decimal places.

METHOD Use the AVERAGE function. Syntax is =AVERAGE(cell ref:cell ref).

Note: In some spreadsheet applications you can shorten the word AVERAGE. Excel does not allow this.

1 In the LOCATION column, select the cell below SEA and key in **AVERAGE** (Figure 4.3).

64	PROPERTIES PER LOCATION	
65	LOCATION	NO OF PROPERTIES
66	COUNTRY	7
67	FOREST	3
68	LAKES	8
69	MOUNTAIN	9
70	RIVERS	5
71	SEA	8
72	AVERAGE	

Figure 4.3 Properties per location – average

2 Enter the formula in cell B72:

=AVERAGE(B66:B71)

Press: **Enter**

3 The answer appears:

70	RIVERS	5
71	SEA	8
72	AVERAGE	6.666666667

4 To display this with no decimal places, click nine times on the Decrease Decimal button until the whole number 7 appears.

INFO

You can also use the **Format** menu, selecting **Cells**, to format cells in a particular way.

Exercise 4   *Price code details section*

Name the range of cells containing the price code and cost per week.

INFO

Excel allows you to give a meaningful name to a cell or to a range of cells. You can then use the name as part of a formula, since Excel will be able to look things up for you in this range. This makes your formulae shorter and easier to understand. It is particularly useful for large spreadsheets or for spreadsheets that are not often used, as it reminds you what the formulae are about.

METHOD 1 Select the range of cells you want to name. In this case C7–G8.
2 From the **Insert** menu, select: **Name**. Click: **Define**.
3 The Define Name dialogue box appears (Figure 4.4).

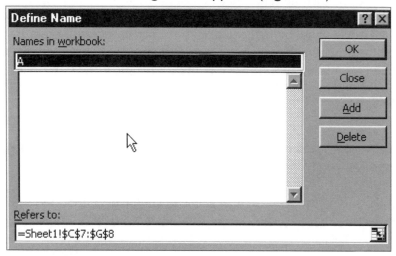

Figure 4.4 Define Name dialogue box

4 In the **Names in workbook** box, enter the name CODE.
  Click on: **OK**.
5 You will notice that the name CODE appears in the Name Box (Figure 4.5).

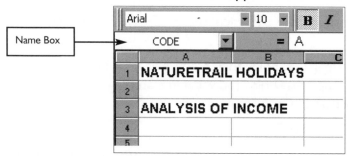

Figure 4.5 Name Box

INFO

Note: We will use this in a formula later.

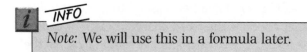

Property details section

Exercise 5

  Calculate the total weeks booked and replicate the formula for each property.

METHOD Use the SUM function to do this.

Exercise 6   *Property details section*

Please calculate the income and replicate the formula for each property. Use the TOTAL WEEKS BOOKED, the PRICE CODE and the FIXED CHARGE. Please note that the FIXED CHARGE should only be applied once per property and not per week booked. The formula must contain the use of the named range together with a LOOKUP function and an absolute cell reference for the FIXED CHARGE. Format this data to two decimal places *without* a £ sign.

METHOD   This is quite a complicated formula, so we need to take each part in turn. Explanations and definitions will be given as they occur.

1 We need to start with the = sign to show it is a formula and follow this by the cell reference for the first property in the TOTAL WEEKS BOOKED column, ie **E18**, so the formula so far is:

=E18

2 We then need to multiply this by the price per week. This is shown in the PRICE CODE DETAILS section of the spreadsheet (the range that we named CODE). Since we have named this range, we can use Excel's LOOKUP function to find the PRICE CODE's corresponding price in £ sterling.

The syntax for the LOOKUP function is =LOOKUP(Cell that holds the compare value, range).

In this case, the cell that holds the compare value is in the PRICE CODE column, cell D18. The range that holds the value in £ sterling is the one we named CODE. Therefore this part of the formula is:

=LOOKUP(D18,CODE)

3 This needs to be multiplied by the first part of the formula, so we now have:

=E18*LOOKUP(D18,CODE)

Note: We only need one = sign in the formula.

4 We now need to add on the FIXED CHARGE. We have been asked that this should be an absolute cell reference. The cell that contains the fixed charge is C10. In order to make this cell address absolute in our formula, we must add a **$** sign in front of the column letter and in front of the row number, so that it becomes: **$C$10**.

(A quick method of doing this, when creating the formula, is by pressing F4 when cell C10 is selected.)

i   *INFO*

An absolute cell reference will not change even if it is replicated or moved to another part of the spreadsheet. By contrast, a relative cell reference will change relatively to its position on the spreadsheet. This happens when you replicate formulae – the cell references change to reflect their new position.

5 Our complete formula now reads:

=E18*LOOKUP(D18,CODE)+$C$10

This gives an INCOME figure for the first property of 4850.

6 Replicate this formula for the other properties.

7 To format these values to two decimal places without a £ sign:

Highlight the cells to format
Click on: the **Increase Decimal** button twice.

INFO

LOOKUP looks in the first row or column of a named cell range. In our example:
- the cell range is C7 to G8 which we have named CODE
- the cell that holds what is being looked for is cell D18 ie B the PRICE CODE
- LOOKUP looks for B in the named cell range and on finding it in cell D7 is able to locate the D value ie £200.00 – the cost per week at price code B.

If the named cell range is wider than it is tall, LOOKUP looks in the first row (as in our example). If the named cell range is square or fatter than it is wide, LOOKUP looks in the first column. LOOKUP will always select the last value in a row or column, so we may have had an incorrect result to our formula if we had had two rows of values, instead of just one.

Using HLOOKUP and VLOOKUP can overcome any problems since HLOOKUP looks in the first row and VLOOKUP in the first column. You can further specify the formula eg if you have more than one column/row of values by adding the column/row reference relative to the named cell range, the formula could look like eg =HLOOKUP(G20,CODE,2).

Exercise 7 Please calculate the total of the INCOME column and format to currency, showing the £ sign and two decimal places.

METHOD Use the SUM function. Format the cell using the 💲 **Currency** button.

Exercise 8 In the TOTAL WEEKS NOT BOOKED column, calculate the total for the first property and replicate the formula for each property. (The maximum number of bookable weeks is 28.)

METHOD This is straightforward.

Exercise 9 Add a column after the TOTAL WEEKS NOT BOOKED column, with the heading LOW(A). You must use this column to indicate whether the bookings are fewer in the BOOKED(A) column than in BOOKED(B) column.

Note: You will need to use the IF function to give the correct message for each property.

If BOOKED(A) is less than BOOKED(B) then LOW(A) will read 'YES'; otherwise it will read 'NO'. Right align the new column heading.

METHOD **I** Enter the column heading in the usual way. Remember to format it as requested, ie right align.

2 You have been asked to use the IF function.

In this case, if BOOKED(A) is less than BOOKED(B) then LOW(A) will read 'YES'; otherwise it will read 'NO'. The formula for this is:

=IF(B18<C18,"YES","NO")

Replicate this formula for the other properties.

Save the spreadsheet. Record the details on the File Store Record Sheet.

Print a copy and fit to one page.

Print a second copy showing the formulae used. Fit to one page and ensure the formulae are shown in full.

3 *Printing graphs*

In this section you will revise and learn:

■ printing spreadsheet extracts, sheets
■ creating and printing graphs.

3.1 *Printing spreadsheet extracts*

Exercise 1 Load the spreadsheet file saved in Section 2. In the PROPERTY DETAILS section, hide only the three columns containing the following headings:

BOOKED(A)
BOOKED(B)
PRICE CODE

Hiding columns

METHOD **1** Select the three columns to hide.
2 From the **Format** menu, select: **Column**, **Hide**.
Note: The same columns in other parts of the spreadsheet are also hidden (Figure 4.6).

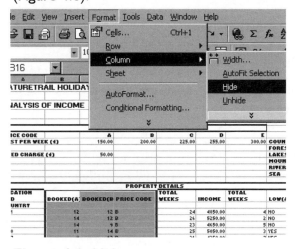

Figure 4.6 Hide

3 You will notice that a thick line appears in place of the hidden columns and the column references are also hidden (Figure 4.7).

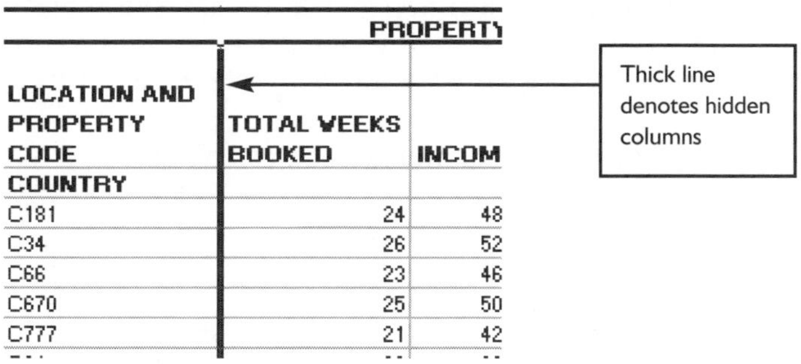

	PROPERTY
LOCATION AND PROPERTY CODE	**TOTAL WEEKS BOOKED**	**INCOM**
COUNTRY		
C181	24	48
C34	26	52
C66	23	46
C670	25	50
C777	21	42

Thick line denotes hidden columns

Figure 4.7 Hiding columns

Exercise 2 Print the PROPERTY DETAILS section with the columns still hidden.

1 Select the area to print.
2 From the **File** menu, select: **Print**.
3 The Print dialogue box appears. In the **Print what** section, click on: **Selection**. Click on: **OK** (Figure 4.8).

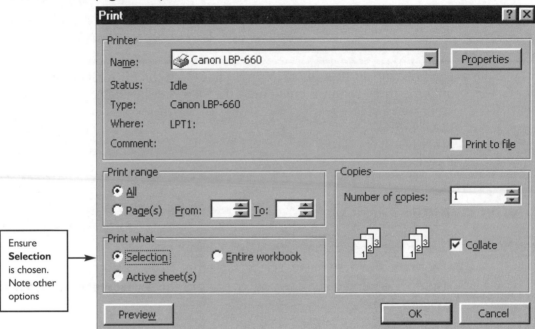

> Ensure
> **Selection**
> is chosen.
> Note other
> options

Figure 4.8 Print dialogue box

Note: You may need to check the Print Preview to ensure it fits one page. If not, adjust the size in **Page Setup**.

Exercise 3 Change the display to show formulae. Produce a printout of the same section (as above) with the same columns still hidden. Ensure all formulae are shown in full.

METHOD

1 Press: **Ctrl + `** (to the left of the number 1 key) to show the formulae.
2 Follow the method shown in the previous exercise.

Note: You will need to change the column widths to show the formulae in full.

Exercise 4 Change the spreadsheet display from formulae back to values and display the previously hidden columns.

METHOD

1 Press: **Ctrl + `** keys to return the formulae back to values.
2 Adjust column widths as necessary.

Unhiding columns

3 To unhide the columns, select the columns on each side of the hidden columns, ie LOCATION AND PROPERTY CODE and TOTAL WEEKS BOOKED.

4 From the **Format** menu, select: **Column**, **Unhide** (Figure 4.9).

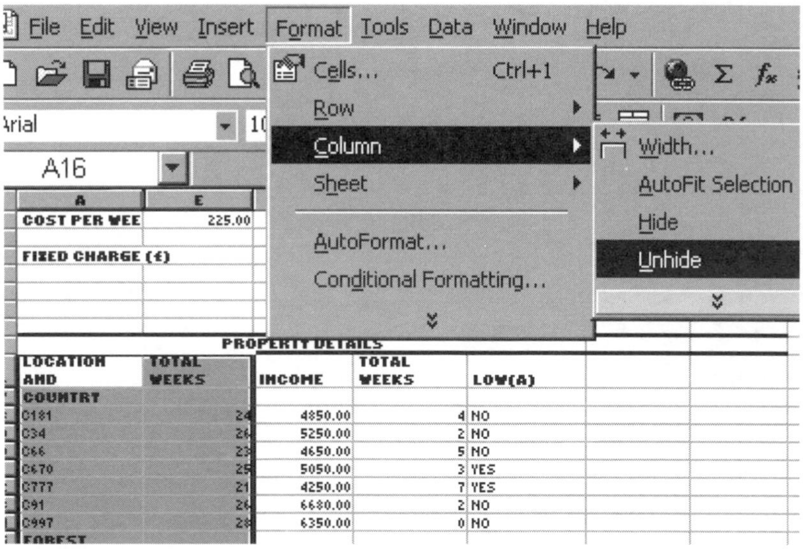

Figure 4.9 Unhide

Exercise 5 Produce the following:

REPORT/EXTRACT

Report format	Group ☐	Column ☐	Tabular ☐

Spreadsheet section	PROPERTIES PER LOCATION

Fields/headings to print	LOCATION, NO OF PROPERTIES

Sort order

Other details
(please specify)

Produce and save separately an extract showing the column headings and the detail in these columns for all 6 locations (including AVERAGE row). To be used later where specified in publication. Do not include the section title in the extract.

Printout required   Yes ☑   No ☐   To be dated   Yes ☐   No ☑

Fit one page   Yes ☑   No ☐   Page numbered   Yes ☐   No ☑

METHOD   **1** Select the area to be printed.
2 From the **Edit** menu, select: **Copy** (Figure 4.10).

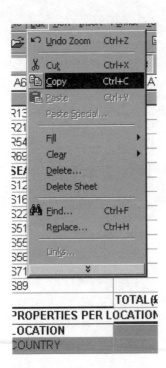

Figure 4.10 Copy

3 Click on: the **New** button to create a new spreadsheet where the extract can be pasted:

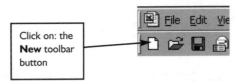

4 From the **Edit** menu, select: **Paste Special...**, the Paste Special dialogue box appears. Ensure **Values** is selected so that the values and not the formulas are copied. Click on: **OK** (Figure 4.11).

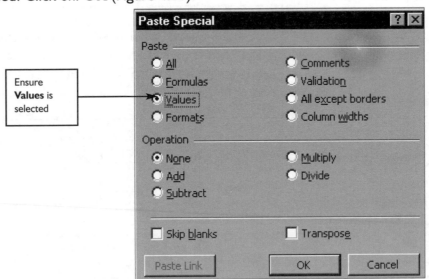

Figure 4.11 Paste Special box

INFO

Paste Special is used when copying cells that have formulae related to them. When they are copied to the new location, they will be unable to access the cells required to produce the formulae results.

5 You will notice that the Average cell has lost its formatting. To rectify this, from the **Edit** menu, select: **Paste Special...**; this time ensure **Formats** is selected. Click on: **OK**.

6 Adjust the cell widths as necessary and save the file with a unique name. Record the details on the File Store Record Sheet.

7 Print the spreadsheet.

Exercise 6 Produce the following:

REPORT/EXTRACT

Report format	Group ☐ Column ☐ Tabular ☐

Spreadsheet section	**PROPERTY DETAILS**

Fields/headings to print Sort order	**LOCATION AND PROPERTY CODE and PRICE CODE**

Other details (please specify)	**Produce an extract showing the details for all properties, in these columns, that have LOW(A) bookings. Do not include the section title in the extract**

Printout required	Yes ✓ No ☐	To be dated	Yes ✓ No ☐
Fit one page	Yes ✓ No ☐	Page numbered	Yes ✓ No ☐

METHOD

1 Hide all the columns in this section except those to print. Hide all the rows that have a NO entry in the LOW(A) column. (Use the same method to hide rows as to hide columns, except from the **Format** menu, select: **Row** not Column.)

2 Add a page number and date to the spreadsheet. (Use **Page Setup**, **Header and Footer** – see the appendix.)

INFO

To save having to unhide all the columns and rows, you can save the spreadsheet before hiding them and then revert back to the saved spreadsheet after printing.

If you do want to unhide the rows/columns, remember you can see where the hidden ones are by looking at the row/column references. The column letters will be missing where there are hidden columns. Similarly, the row numbers will be missing where there are hidden rows.

3.2 Creating and printing graphs

Exercise 7

Create a graph from the spreadsheet following the instructions below:

GRAPH

Title | COMPARISON OF BOOKED(A) AND BOOKED(B)

Other details (please specify) | Based on Bookings. Compare BOOKED(A) and BOOKED(B) for each location

Printout required   Yes ✓ No ☐   Legend required   Yes ✓ No ☐

Axes labels required Yes ✓ No ☐   Type: bar/column ☐ Line ✓ Pie ☐

METHOD   This is a straightforward graph and will provide useful revision. Ensure you follow the instructions carefully. (Refer to the quick reference guide on page 00 if you cannot remember how to produce a graph).

Exercise 8

Follow the instructions below:

GRAPH

Title | COMPARISON OF BOOKED(A) AND BOOKED(B)

Other details (please specify) | The wrong type of graph was requested, please change it. Retain the Y axis minimum value of 0 and increase the maximum to 150. Set intermediate values to intervals of 30. To be used where specified in the presentation.

Printout required   Yes ✓ No ☐   Legend required   Yes ✓ No ☐

Axes labels required Yes ✓ No ☐   Type: bar/column ✓ Line ☐ Pie ☐

METHOD   I With the line graph displayed, right-click on the graph; a menu appears. Click on: **Chart Type...** (Figure 4.12).

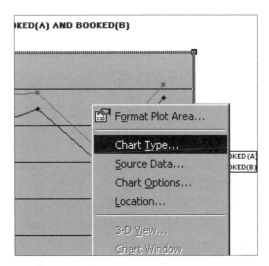

Figure 4.12 Chart Type ...

2 The Chart Type dialogue box appears. Click on: **Column** and then **OK** (Figure 4.13).

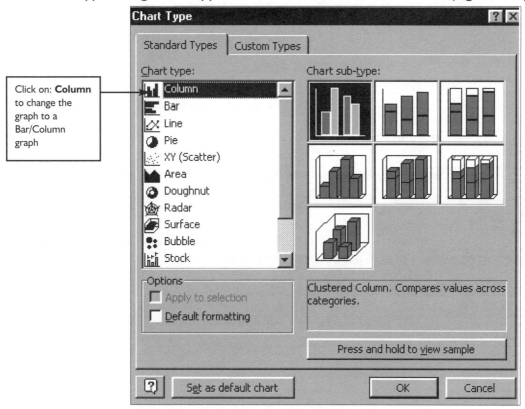

Figure 4.13 Chart Type dialogue box

3 To change the Y-axis values, double-click on: the **Value Axis** (Figure 4.14).

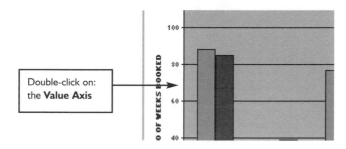

Figure 4.14 Value Axis

4 The Format Axis dialogue box appears.

5 With the **Scale** tab selected, change the Maximum value to 150 and the Major unit to 30. Click: **OK** (Figure 4.15).

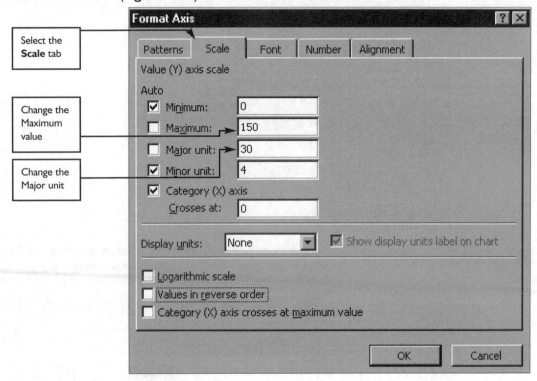

Figure 4.15 Format Axis dialogue box

6 Record the details on the File Store Record Sheet, making a note that this graph will be used in the presentation.

Chart labels can be displayed alongside bars/columns in charts:
- At Step 3 of Chart Wizard, select the **Data Labels** tab
- Click in the **Show value** option button.

Excel quick reference for IBT III

Action	Keyboard	Mouse	Right-mouse menu	Menu
Align cell entries	Select cells to align			
		Click: the relevant button: ≣ ≡ ≣ ▦	**Format Cells** Select the **Alignment** tab Select from the **Horizontal:** drop-down menu as appropriate	F**ormat, C**e**lls**
Absolute cell reference	Add **$** sign in front of the cell reference column letter and in front of the cell reference row number or press: **F4**			
Bold text	Select cells to embolden			
	Ctrl + B	Click: the **B** **Bold** button	**Format Cells** Select the **Font** tab Select **Bold** from the **Font style:** menu	F**ormat, C**e**lls**
Capitals (blocked)	**Caps Lock** (Press again to remove)			
Close a file	**Ctrl + W**	Click: the ☒ **Close** button		**File, Close**
Columns, adding	Select the column following the one where you want the new column to appear – by clicking on the column ref box (at top of column)			
			Insert	**Insert, Columns**
Columns, changing width of		Drag the column border C ↔ D	Select the column(s) by clicking (and dragging) on the column ref box (at top of column)	
		to fit the widest entry	**Column Width** Key in the width you want	F**ormat, C**olumn, **Width** Key in the width you want *OR* F**ormat, C**olumn, **AutoFit Selection**
Columns, deleting	Select the column you want to delete by clicking on the column ref box (at top of column)			
	Delete		**Delete**	**Edit, Delete**
Copy (replicate) formulae	Select cell with formula to be copied Drag the mouse from bottom right corner of cell over cells to copy to, release mouse			
Create a new file	**Ctrl + N**	Click: the ▢ **New** button		**File, New**
Date, adding	From the **View** menu, select: **Header and Footer** Click: **Custom Header** Click: where you want the date to appear Click: the ▦ **Date** button			

Action	Keyboard	Mouse	Right-mouse menu	Menu
Decimal places		Click: the ⁺.₀₀ **Increase Decimal** button to increase the number of decimal places Click: the .₀₀⁺ **Decrease Decimal** button to decrease the number of decimal places	**Format Cells** Select the **Number** tab Click: **Number** in the **Category:** menu Select the number of decimal places you need	**Format, Cells**
Enter formulae	Click: in the cell where you want the result to appear Key in: = followed by the formula Press: **Enter**			
Enter numeric data	Click: in the cell where you want the number to appear Key in: the data Press: **Enter**			
Enter text	Click: in the cell where you want text to appear Key in: the text Press: **Enter**			
Exit the program		Click: the ☒ **Close** button		**File, Exit**
Fit to page				**File, Page Setup, Fit to (1) Page**
Formulae, functions	Click on the cell where the result is required Use: **=SUM(cell ref:cell ref)** for adding a range of cells *OR* Click the: **Σ AutoSum** button Click and drag over the cell range Press: **Enter** Use: **=AVERAGE(cell ref:cell ref)** to find the average value in a range of cells Use: **=COUNT(cell ref:cell ref)** to count the number of cells in range Use: **=LOOKUP(cell that holds the compare value, range)** to find the cell that contains the value specified Use: **=IF(test,"value if true", "value if false")** to return a value for the given test			
Formulae, operators	**+** add **-** subtract ***** multiply **/** divide			
Formulae, printing	Ensure the formulae are showing in full			
				File, Page Setup, Page tab, **Landscape** *OR* **File, Page Setup, Page** tab Under **Scaling**, select **Fit to 1 page wide** and **1 page tall**
Formulae, showing	**Ctrl + `**			**Tools, Options, View** Under **Window options**, select **Formulas** so that a tick appears

Action	Keyboard	Mouse	Right-mouse menu	Menu
Help	**F1** **Shift + F1**			**H**elp **Microsoft Excel Help** **What's This?**
Hide columns	**Ctrl + O**		**H**ide	F**o**rmat, **C**olumn, **H**ide
Hide rows			**H**ide	F**o**rmat, **R**ow, **H**ide
Integers (whole numbers)		Click: the [.00 →.0] **Decrease Decimal** button until you have reduced the number of decimal places to zero	**Format Cells** Select the **Number** tab Click: **Number** in the **Category:** menu Change the number of decimal places to zero	F**o**rmat, **C**e**l**ls
Move to end of document	**Ctrl + End**	Use scroll bars		
Move to top of document	**Ctrl + Home**	Use scroll bars		
Moving around	Use the cursor keys	Click: where you want to move to		
Naming cells	From the **Insert** menu, select: **Name**, **Define** Key in: the name Click: **OK**			
Open an existing file	**Ctrl + O**	Click: the [📂] **Open** button		**F**ile, **O**pen
	Select: the drive required Select: the filename Click: **OK**			
Page number, adding	From the **View** menu, select: **Header and Footer** Click: **Custom Header** Click: where you want the date to appear Click: the [#] **Page** button			
Page Setup	From the **File** menu, select: **Page Setup** Choose from **Margins**, **Paper size**, **Paper Source**, **Layout**			
Print file	**Ctrl + P** Select the options you need Press: **Enter**	Click: the [🖨] **Print** button		**F**ile, **P**rint Select the options you need and click **OK**
Print preview		Click: the [🔍] **Print Preview** button		**F**ile, **Print Pre**_v_**iew**
Printing in Landscape	From the **File** menu, select: **Page Set**u**p** Click: the **Page** tab Select: **Landscape** Click: **OK**			
Printing selected cells only	Select the cells to print			
	Ctrl + P Select: **Selection** Click: **OK**			**F**ile, **P**rint

Action	Keyboard	Mouse	Right-mouse menu	Menu
Remove text emphasis	Select text to be changed			
	Ctrl + B (remove bold) **Ctrl + I** (remove italics) **Ctrl + U** (remove underline)	Click: the appropriate button: **B** *I* **U**	**Format Cells** Select the **Font** tab Click: **Regular** in the **Font Style:** menu	**Format**, **Cells**
Replicate (copy) formulae	Select: the cell with the formula to be copied Drag the mouse from the bottom right corner of the cell over the cells to copy to Release mouse			
Restore deleted input	**Ctrl + Z**	Click: the ↺ **Undo** button		**Edit**, **Undo**
Rows, adding	Select the row by clicking in the row ref box (at side of row)			
			Insert	**Insert**, **Rows**
Rows, deleting	Select the row by clicking in the row ref box (at side of row)			
			Delete	**Edit**, **Delete**
Save	**Ctrl + S**	Click: the 🖫 **Save** button		**File**, **Save**
	If you have not already saved the file you will be prompted to specify the directory and to name the file. If you have already done this, then Excel will automatically save it.			
Save using a different name or to a different directory				**File**, **Save As**
	Select the appropriate drive and change the filename if relevant. Click: **Save**			
Selecting cells	Click and drag across cells			
Remove selection	Click in any white space			
Spell check	Move cursor to top of document			
	F7	Click: the ✓ **Spelling** button		**Tools**, **Spelling**
Unhide columns	Select the columns on either side of the hidden ones			
	Ctrl + Shift + 0		**Unhide**	**Format**, **Column**, **Unhide**
Unhide rows	Select the rows on either side of the hidden ones			
			Unhide	**Format**, **Row**, **Unhide**

Hints and tips

- *Using Autofill:* If the cell contains a number, date or time period that can extend in a series, by dragging the fill handle of a cell you can copy that cell to other cells in the same row or column. The values are incremented. For example, if the cell contains MONDAY, you can quickly fill in other cells in a row or column with TUESDAY, WEDNESDAY and so on.

METHOD

1 Key in the first label or if numbers key in the first two numbers.
2 Select the cell(s) containing the label or numbers you entered.
3 Move the mouse over the bottom right corner of the selected cell(s).
4 Press and hold down the left mouse and drag over the cells you want to include in the series.
5 Release the mouse.

You must not have a cell active whilst trying to format it.

- *Using Fit to Page:* Having problems printing on one page, even with a landscape setting (this may happen when printing formulae)? Use Fit to Page.

  From the **File** menu, select: **Page Setup**, **Page** tab, **Scaling** section – **Fit to 1 page**.

- Check the formulae you have used – are they generating the correct results? It is a good idea to check the first formula, in a range, with a calculator (or longhand). (*Note*: There may be a small discrepancy between the results due to rounding by the spreadsheet.)

- Ensure you have followed the alignment and formatting instructions.

- After replicating formulae, delete any zero or erroneous values in cells where they should not be.

Important! Check your work carefully. All numeric data must be 100% correct in spreadsheet assignments.

Charts using Excel quick reference for IBT III

Action	Keyboard	Mouse	Right-mouse menu	Menu
Create a chart	Select the data to chart			
		Click: the 📊 **Chart Wizard** button		**Insert**, **Chart**

	STEP 1 Select: the chart type
	    Click: **Next**
	STEP 2 Check that the source data is correct, if not change it
	    Click: **Next**
	STEP 3 Select: the **Titles** tab
	    Key in the titles
	    Select: the **Legend** tab
	    Click: in the **Show legend** box to add/remove tick as appropriate
	    Select: the **Data Labels** tab
	    Click: **Show label/Show value** as appropriate
	    Click: **Next**
	STEP 4 Click: **As new sheet:**
	    Key in: the chart name
	    Click: **Finish**			

Action	Keyboard	Mouse	Right-mouse menu	Menu
Print a chart	With the chart displayed on screen			
	Ctrl + P Ensure **Active sheet** is selected. Click: **OK**	Click: the 🖨 **Print** button (This will automatically print the sheet)		**File**, **Print** Ensure **Active sheet** is selected. Click: **OK**
Save a chart	**Ctrl + S**	Click: the 💾 **Save** button		**File**, **Save**
Change graphical display	*To change the scale ratios:* With the graph on screen Select: the **Plot Area** Drag the corner handles inwards (to reduce the scale) and outwards (to increase the scale) *To set upper and lower limits for Y (vertical) axis:* With the graph on screen Double-click: the **Value Axis** In the **Format Axis** dialogue box: Click: the **Scale** tab Key in: the new values in the **Maximum** and **Minimum** boxes Click: **OK** *To set intermediate values:* With the graph on screen Double-click: the **Value Axis** In the **Format Axis** dialogue box: Click: the **Scale** tab Change the **Major** unit to the required value Click: **Close**			

Hints and tips

■ **Reloading a saved chart**: Reload the spreadsheet from which the chart was produced. Click on: the **Chart name** tab at the bottom of the sheet.

■ When you change data in the spreadsheet, the data on the corresponding chart will change automatically to incorporate the amended data.

■ Have you selected the required data to graph?

■ Have you labelled it as requested?

■ Have you controlled the Y axis as specified?

Chapter 5

Automated presentation production using PowerPoint

1 Getting started

In this section you will learn how to:
- understand PowerPoint basics
- load PowerPoint
- create a new presentation
  - create slides
  - choose layouts
  - format and align text
  - save the presentation
  - insert, resize and reposition graphics
  - implement a colour scheme
  - spellcheck
- print a presentation
  - one slide per page
  - miniatures
  - notes
- exit PowerPoint.

1.1 Understanding PowerPoint basics

PowerPoint enables you to create, organise and design effective presentations. These can be used as handouts, overhead transparencies, 35 mm slides and automated presentations on a computer. We will be concentrating on automated presentations in this chapter but, as you work through the exercises, you will become aware of other options available through the menu systems.

PowerPoint is easy to learn and use if you know the basics of other Microsoft packages, eg Word, Excel. This section will enable you to gain a quick feel of PowerPoint basics before progressing to more IBT task-focused exercises.

1.2 Loading PowerPoint

Load PowerPoint.

METHOD 1

1 In the Windows 98 desktop, click on: the **Start** button – a menu appears.
2 Select: **Programs** by moving the mouse over it – another menu appears (Figure 5.1).
3 Select: **Microsoft PowerPoint** (Figure 5.1).

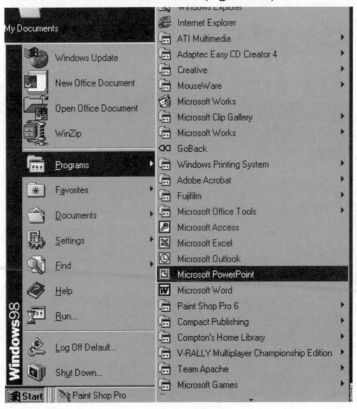

Figure 5.1 Programs – PowerPoint

METHOD 2

(Use if you have a shortcut icon to PowerPoint on your desktop.) In the Windows 98 desktop, click on: the **Microsoft PowerPoint** shortcut icon:

Either method results in the PowerPoint window being displayed on screen (Figure 5.2).

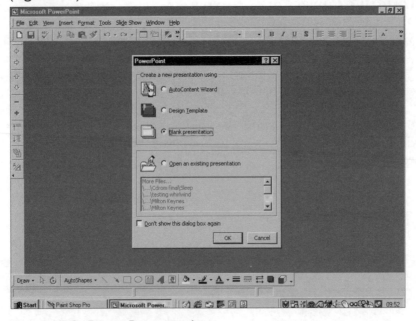

Figure 5.2 PowerPoint window

1.3   *Creating a new presentation*

Exercise 2 Create slide 1.

Note: PowerPoint uses the word 'slide' for each page created, even for the production of paper printouts or overhead transparencies.

METHOD 1 Click on: **Blank Presentation** and **OK**. The New Slide dialogue box appears (Figure 5.3).

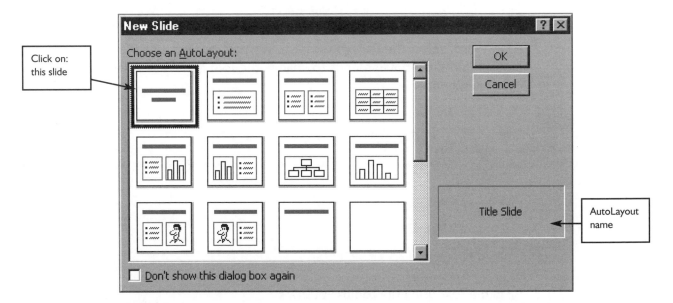

Figure 5.3 New Slide dialogue box

2 There are many different layouts to choose. In this case click the slide layout at the top left (it may already be chosen). Click on: **OK**.
3 This slide is now ready for your input (Figure 5.4).

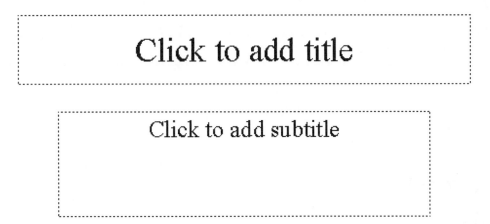

Figure 5.4 Slide ready for input

4 In the slide window, click on: the top placeholder (Click to add title) and key in **Learning PowerPoint**.
5 Click on: the bottom placeholder (click to add sub-title) and key in your name.

> **INFO**
>
> Title and subtitle can also be referred to as heading and subheading. Body text is usually the text that follows the subheading.

Exercise 3 Format the text on slide 1

METHOD   1   Ensure that the Formatting toolbar is visible (shown below). If not, from the **View** menu, select: **Toolbars** then **Formatting**.

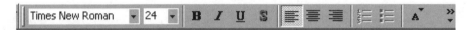

2   As in Word, select the text you want to format and then use the Formatting toolbar buttons and drop-down menus to change the font type, point size, embolden, italicise and underline.

> **INFO**
>
> ### Serif and sans serif fonts
>
> Serifs are small lines that stem from the upper and lower ends of characters. Serif fonts have such lines. Sans serif fonts do not have these lines. As a general rule, larger text in a sans serif font and body text in a serif font usually makes for easier reading. For example:
>
> **Times New Roman** is a serif font
> **Arial** is a sans serif font.

3   Align the text using the toolbar buttons.
4   Change the font colour by clicking the down arrow on the ☒ **Font Color** button on the **Drawing** toolbar. (By default this toolbar is at the bottom of the working area. If this is not visible, from the **View** menu, select: **Toolbars** and then **Drawing**.)

Saving the presentation

Exercise 4 Save the presentation.

METHOD   From the **File** menu, select: **Save As**. Choose where you want to save the file and key in a filename. Click on: **Save**.

Creating slide 2

Exercise 5 Create a second slide in the presentation.

METHOD   1   Click on: the 🖻 **New Slide** button on the toolbar.
2   Choose the Text and Clip Art layout as shown. Click on: **OK** (Figure 5.5).

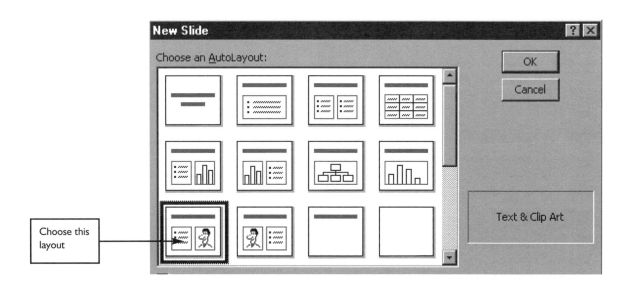

Choose this layout

Figure 5.5 New Slide – layout

3 In the **Click to add title** placeholder, key in **Bullets and Graphics**.
4 In the left-hand placeholder, key in the numbers 1–7, pressing **Enter** after each number except 7 (the last one). Notice that a bulleted list has been created.
5 To insert a graphical image in the right-hand placeholder, double-click in the placeholder.
6 Click on a **Clip Art** category to view Clip Art. If there is no Clip Art in that category, click on the **Back** button. Click on another category.
7 Scroll through **Clip Art** to decide which one to use.
8 Click on the chosen one and then click on: **Insert**.
Slide 2 will now look something like Figure 5.6.

Bullets and Graphics

- 1
- 2
- 3
- 4
- 5
- 6
- 7

Resize the graphic by dragging the handles

Figure 5.6 Slide 2

9 Resize the graphical image by dragging the handles.

 INFO

If you want to preserve the proportions (aspect ratio) of the image always resize from a corner.

Moving the elements of the slide

Reduce the size of the graphic and reposition it at the right-hand corner of the slide.

METHOD
1 Click on the graphic to select it.
2 Reduce the size as in **9** above.
3 With the graphic still selected, and holding down the left mouse button over it, drag it to the required position.

 INFO

This repositioning can be carried out on any of the elements following the same method, but you will notice that you need to point the mouse at the border of some of the elements before the arrowhead cross appears. When this appears you can move the element.

Your slide will look something like Figure 5.7.

Bullets and Graphics

- 1
- 2
- 3
- 4
- 5
- 6
- 7

Figure 5.7 Slide – repositioning elements

4 Save your work using the toolbar button method.

Creating slide 3

Create slide 3 for the presentation using the blank layout. Decide on your own text for this slide.

METHOD
1 Click on: the **New Slide** button.
2 Choose the **Blank** layout this time.
3 Experiment with adding your own text and graphics.

To add text

METHOD 1 Cick on: the **Text Box** button from the Drawing toolbar. (If this is not visible, from the **View** menu, select: **Toolbars** then **Drawing**.)

2 Click where you want the text to start.

Note: You need not drag out a box, as the text will expand the box to fit.

3 Key in the text and format it as required.
4 Click in any white space on the slide when finished.

To add graphics

1 From the **Insert** menu, select: **Picture** then **Clip Art** (Figure 5.8).

Figure 5.8 Clip Art

> **INFO**
>
> Notice that the menu shows other types of picture you can insert. We will look at some of these later.

2 Right-click the Clip Art you want to insert. Select: **Insert**.
3 Close the Insert Clip Art box.

Note: The graphic is placed in the centre of the slide. Resize and reposition it as necessary following the method given above. Be careful not to superimpose (overlap) any of the elements – resize and reposition them so that they do not overlap.

Use your imagination and practise adding and changing elements on this slide. When you are happy with the result, save your work. You now have three slides in the presentation.

Viewing the slides

> **INFO**
>
> There are several ways to view your slides. The buttons at the bottom left of the window are for selecting the different options:
>
>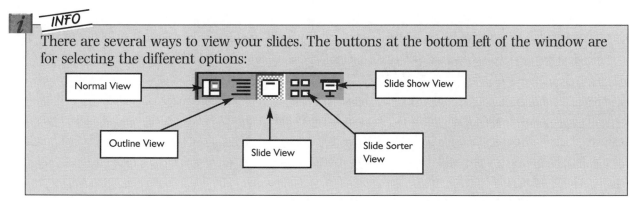

- *Normal View* – contains three panes: Outline, Slide and Notes. The pane sizes can be adjusted by dragging the pane borders. **Normal View** displays slides individually and can be used to work on/view all parts of your presentation. The Outline pane gives an overview of your presentation. The Notes pane allows you to input any notes that you want to make about the slide. Use this view or **Slide View** to create/edit slides.

- *Outline View* – displays an outline of your presentation, You can enter/review the text in your presentation in this view.

- *Slide View* – displays one slide at a time. Use this view or **Normal View** to create/edit slides:

- *Slide Sorter View*
  - you can view all your slides in this view as miniatures (small versions or thumbnails)
  - zoom in and out for more/less detail using **Zoom** Control
  - sort slides into a different presentation order by clicking on the slide you want to move and dragging it to a new location
  - add a new slide by placing the pointer between the slides where you want the new slide to appear and clicking on the **New Slide** toolbar button
  - delete a slide by selecting it and pressing the **Delete** key. Use the **Undo** toolbar button to reinstate the deleted slide.

- *Slide Show View* – shows your slides on a full screen, as they will appear when you set a slide show in motion. Select the first slide. Click the **Slide Show** button. To view the next slide, press: **Page Down**. When all the slides have been viewed you will be returned to the previous view.

Practise with the different views now.

Implementing a colour scheme

Exercise 8 Change the background colour to light blue and the title text to red.

METHOD

I In Slide View, from the **Format** menu, select: **Slide Color Scheme**. The Color Scheme dialogue box appears. The default here is Standard and you can experiment with the colour schemes provided. However, to create your own scheme, ensure **Custom** is selected, click on: **Background**, then **Change Color** (Figure 5.9).

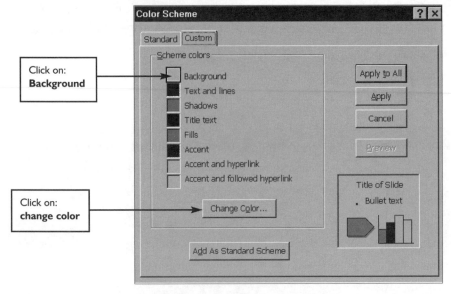

Figure 5.9 Color Scheme dialogue box

2 The Background Color dialogue box appears. With **Standard** selected, click on: a shade of light blue, then **OK** (Figure 5.10).

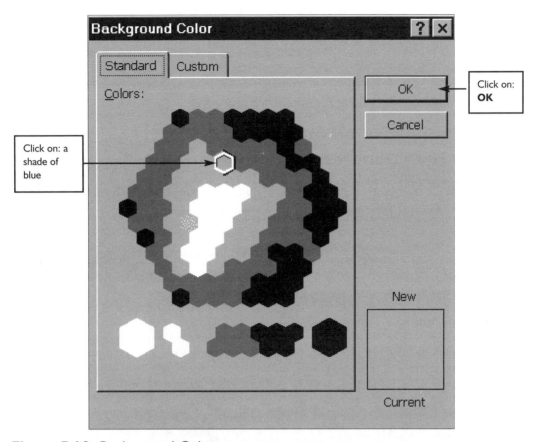

Figure 5.10 Background Color

3 You are returned to the Color Scheme dialogue box. This time select **Text** and **Lines** and follow the instructions above, choosing the colour red for the Title text.
4 When you are returned to the Colour Scheme dialogue box, click on: **Apply to All**. You are automatically returned to your slide.
   Note: You could have chosen to apply to only one slide.
5 Change to Slide Sorter View to see how your slides look with this colour scheme.
   Note: You will notice that the **Title** text is unchanged. To change the **Title text**, select: **Title text** from the Colour Scheme dialogue box.
   Save your work.

Spellcheck the presentation

Exercise 9   Spellcheck the presentation.

METHOD   Click on: the **Spelling** button. The spellcheck is consistent with other Office applications. Always resave your work after spellchecking to save any corrections.

INFO

Use a light background when you are printing a slide; it is easier to read. Dark backgrounds work well with an automated slide show. You can apply a design to your slide show (**Format** menu, **Apply Design**). Experiment with this later but for the purposes of IBT III, bearing in mind that the assignment must be completed in a set time, it is better to stick with the basics you can manipulate yourself.

1.4 Printing your presentation

Exercise 10 Print the presentation of three slides, one slide per page.

METHOD From the **File** menu, select: **Print**. The Print – Basics dialogue box appears (Figure 5.11).

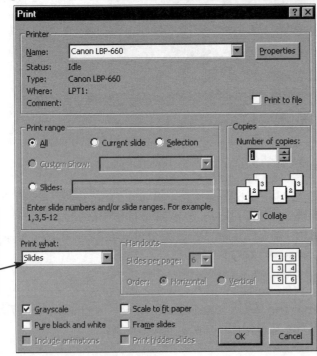

With the Slides option selected here, each slide will print on its own page

Figure 5.11 Print – Basics dialogue box

Exercise 11 Print the presentation as miniatures (thumbnails) on one page.

METHOD
1 From the **File** menu, select: **Print**. The Print – Basics dialogue box appears (as in Figure 5.11).
2 In the **Print what** box, click on: the **down arrow** and select: **Handouts** (six per page).
3 In the **Handouts** section, select: **Slides per page 6**.
4 Click on: **OK**.

INFO

By choosing six slides per page (we only have three slides so far) the slides will print without leaving lines for notes.

You can also choose **Notes** Pages from the **Print what** box.

1.5 *Exiting PowerPoint*

METHOD From the **File** menu, select: **Exit**.

2 *Master slide, importing, copyfitting, slide order*

In this section you will learn how to:
- set up a master slide
- import images and extracts
- copyfit material
- set up/change slide order.

2.1 *Setting up a master slide*

In order that your slides give a common feel to a presentation, it is a good idea to set up a master slide containing common elements that will appear on all the slides. These elements cannot then be deleted, except from the master slide. Setting up a master slide is essential for the IBT III assignment.

Exercise

Set up a master slide with the following specifications:

To contain the graphic file **Logo** (this file is stored on the accompanying disk), the name of the organisation Naturetrail Holidays, the name of the designer (your name) and the date. Any text on the master slide should be between 12 and 16 pt and any typeface can be chosen.

METHOD
1. Load PowerPoint.
2. Select: **Blank presentation** and click on: **OK**.
3. Select: **Blank slide** and click on: **OK**.
4. From the View menu, select: **Master**, **Slide Master**. The Master slide appears (Figure 5.12).

 INFO

You could work with some of the elements of this master slide but, as a personal preference, I find it easier to delete its contents and insert my own. You then have more control over the layout.

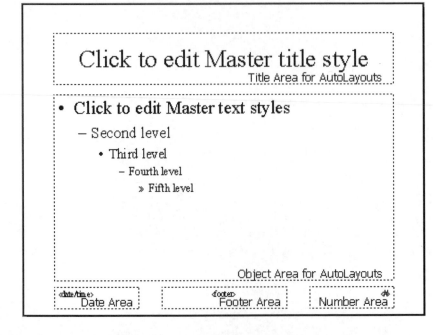

Figure 5.12 Master slide

5 Delete all the elements on the master slide: select each one by clicking on the frame of an element and press: **Delete**.

6 Insert a text box for the name of the organisation **Naturetrail Holidays** (click on: the **Text Box** button on the **Drawing** toolbar and click on the slide where you want the text to appear). Ensure you have selected the requested point size of between 12 to 16, then key in the text.

INFO

You may not be able to read this size of text without zooming in. Using the **Toolbar Zoom**, change to a size which is comfortable for you. Change back to view the whole slide.

7 Repeat for your name and for the date.

8 Rearrange these elements so they look pleasing to the eye. Remember that the main text for each slide will be placed in the centre, so it is a good idea to place them near the edges of the slide (Figure 5.13).

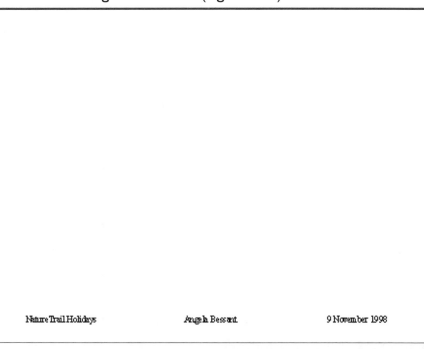

Figure 5.13 Rearranging the slide's elements

Inserting a graphic

METHOD I From the **Insert** menu, select: **Picture, From File...** (Figure 5.14).

Figure 5.14 Picture, From File ...

2 The Insert Picture dialogue box appears. Select the drive and filename and click on: **Insert**.
3 Reduce the size of the graphic and position it on the slide.
4 The master slide is now complete and will look something like the one in Figure 5.15.
5 Return to **Slide** View.

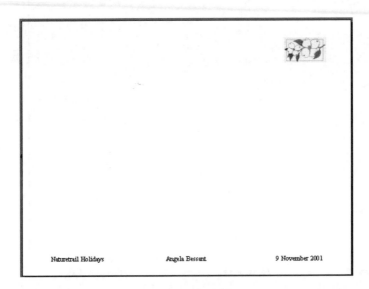

Figure 5.15 The completed slide

Note: If requested you can add drawing elements to the master slide. Use the Drawing toolbar buttons eg to create a line above the text in Figure 5.15.

i INFO

When you choose a new slide in the presentation it will be based on the master slide you have just created.

INFO

For IBT III you are given a specification for the presentation – you have two House Style Sheets and a Design Brief. Examples of these are given here and you should study them well before carrying out the following exercises. These exercises will take you through the necessary stages to complete the presentation.

Exercise 2   Save the presentation ready for use in the next part of this section i.e. the master slide has been created to suit the following exercises.

Design Brief: content of the presentation slides

Create a master slide. Please refer to the House Style Sheets to ensure this adheres to Naturetrail Holidays' conventions and for information on slide layout and effects. The text for the automated presentation is given below. You must retain case as shown.

Important! You must create a master slide to be used as a background for all five slides.

Text for automated presentation

Slide No.	Type of entry	Slide content	Slide duration
Master slide	Master slide text	Specified text and image – see House Style Sheet 2: Slide layout and effects, for details	
Slide 1	Heading	WANT TO UNWIND?	5–10 secs
	Heading	PUT US IN MIND!	
Slide 2	Heading	NATURETRAIL HOLIDAYS	7–15 secs
	Heading	TOTAL RELAXATION	
	Subheading	Tel: 01234 29786	
	Subheading	Open 7 to 7	
Slide 3	Heading	DELIGHTFUL LOCATIONS	15–20 secs
	Body text	Our holiday homes are situated in some of the most beautiful settings, for example:	
	Bullet text	Mountains Lakes Sea	
Slide 4	Heading	BOOKINGS	15–25 secs
	Body text	Why not take a holiday early in the year when there is usually more choice:	
	Graph	*Insert graph here*	
Slide 5	Heading	CONTACT US NOW!	15–20 secs
	Heading	WE'LL BE HAPPY TO HELP	
	Subheading	Loyalty Savings	
	Extract text	*Extract text from text file as specified in Design Brief*	

House Style Sheet 1: Presentation text styles

Style name	Typeface	Point size	Feature	Alignment	Additional
Master slide	Any	Between 12 and 16	Any	–	All master slide text must be the same style and consistent throughout the presentation
Heading	Sans serif	Between 40 and 60	Bold	Centre	Consistent throughout the presentation
Subheading	Sans serif	Between 26 and 36	Italic	Centre	Consistent throughout the presentation
Body text	Sans serif	Between 18 and 24	None	Left	Consistent throughout presentation
Bullet text	Sans serif	Between 18 and 24	Any	Left	No more than six bullet points per slide
Extract text	Sans serif	Between 18 and 24	Italic	Left	Consistent throughout the presentation. **Do not** apply to any text included in imported image or graph

Copyfitting
- Text and imported data are adjusted so that they are not superimposed on other text or data.
- Imported data must not be split across slides.

House Style Sheet 2: Presentation slide layout and effects

Feature	Colour	Style	Position	Max number	Additional
Background	Any	Any	–	One	Consistent use throughout the presentation
Data on master slide	Any – see Additional column	–	–	Two text colours	Consistent use throughout the presentation Ensure legibility against background colour/style To contain the organisation's logo, the name of the organisation, name of designer and the date
Text	Any – see Additional column	–	–	Two colours	Consistent use throughout the presentation Ensure legibility against background colour/style
Logo	Corporate colours or black-and-white	–	Master slide	–	Consistent use throughout the presentation and original proportions maintained
Images, diagrams or graphs	Any	–	As specified in Design Brief	As specified in Design Brief	Original proportions must be maintained at all times
Transitions	–	–	–	Four effects	At least two different effects must be used
Builds	–	–	–	Four effects	At least two different effects must be used

2.2 Creating slides and copyfitting material

Note: For the following exercises you will need to use the Design Brief and House Style Sheet 1 – Presentation text styles.

Exercise 3 Create slide 1 as per specification.

METHOD
1 Click on: the **New Slide** button.
2 Refer to the Design Brief and House Style Sheet 1 and choose a slide that most resembles the slide you are producing.
   Note: If there is not a slide format that resembles the one you want, choose: **Blank slide**.
3 Click on: **OK**.

> **INFO**
> The Design Brief requests that this slide is to contain two headings. House Style Sheet 1 gives details of the formatting of the text, ie typeface – sans serif point size – 40 to 60, feature – bold, alignment – centre.

4 Enter the text and format it as above.
   Note: It is important that you match the case of the text.
   Ensure you make a note of the point size and font you have chosen for the headings as this must be consistent throughout the presentation. I have chosen the sans serif font Arial, point size 44.
5 It will look something like Figure 5.16.

Figure 5.16 Slide 1

> **INFO**
> Ensure you make the spacing between lines within a style area consistent throughout the slides.

Exercise 4 Create slides **2 and** 3 using the same steps as for slide 1. (They will look similar to Figure 5.17.)

NATURETRAIL HOLIDAYS

TOTAL RELAXATION

Tel: 01234 29786
Open 7 to 7

Slide 2

DELIGHTFUL LOCATIONS

Our holiday homes are situated in some of the most beautiful settings, for example:

- Mountains
- Lakes
- Sea

Slide 3

Figure 5.17 Slides 2 and 3

Importing a graph

Exercise 5 Create slide 4, inserting the graph saved in Chapter 4, Section 3.

METHOD 1 Using the Chart slide template as shown in Figure 5.18, enter the text for this slide.

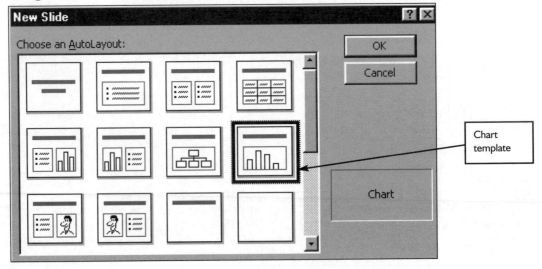

Figure 5.18 Chart slide template

2   Your slide will now look similar to the one in Figure 5.19.

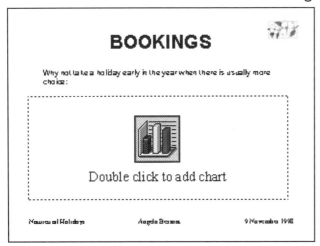

Figure 5.19 Slide 4 – text

3   Load Excel and load the saved graph to insert.
4   Ensure the graph is selected by clicking it (handles appear on the border of the chart area).
5   Click on: the **Copy** button.
6   Switch back to the PowerPoint window by clicking on the **PowerPoint** file on the taskbar.
7   Click on: the **Paste** button. The graph appears on the slide.
8   Close Excel from the taskbar (right-click on Microsoft Excel and click on: **Close**).
9   Resize the graph so it does not overlap other elements on the slide.
10   Slide 4 will now look similar to the one shown in Figure 5.20.

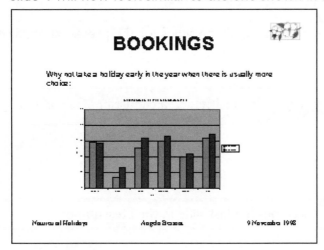

Figure 5.20 Slide 4 completed

Note: It is not essential that this slide template is used when importing a graph.

Exercise 6   Create slide 5.
Note: This slide is to contain text that has been extracted from a text file – this file can be found on the accompanying disk.
The extract text is in the fourth paragraph. Use only the sentence beginning '**We will be continuing...**' and ending '**...super cash prizes**'.

Inserting extract text

METHOD

1 Create the slide in the usual way.
2 Load Word and load the file that contains the extract text.
3 Select the extract text and click on: the **Copy** button.
4 Switch back to the PowerPoint window by clicking on the **PowerPoint** file on the taskbar.
5 Drag a text box to accommodate the text on to the slide and click on: the **Paste** button.
6 Close the Word file from the taskbar.
7 Format the text as requested.
8 The slide will look similar to the one shown in Figure 5.21.

Figure 5.21 Slide 5 with extracted text

Note: You have now completed all the slides for the presentation. Save the presentation.

i INFO

It is worth saving the file after each slide has been created just in case something goes wrong.

Changing slide order

Exercise 7   Move slide 1 so that it becomes the last slide in the presentation.

METHOD

1 Change to **Slide Sorter** View.
2 Point and hold down the left mouse button on slide 1 and drag the slide to the required position.
3 Resave the presentation.

Exercise 8   Spellcheck the presentation.

Exercise 9   Print a copy of each slide *and* an overview on one page containing a miniature (thumbnail) of each slide.

Exercise 10   Change the slides back to their original order, ie move the last slide so that it becomes slide 1 in the presentation.

Exercise 11   Resave the presentation.

METHOD   Follow the method given above.

3 Transitional timings and effects, automated presentations, build effects

In this section you will learn how to:
- create transitional timings
- run an automated presentation
- create transitional effects
- create build effects
- loop a presentation.

3.1 Creating transitional timings

 INFO

In Slide Show View you can see how the slides look on a full screen by moving to the next/previous slide using the **Page Up/Page Down** keys (other keys will also perform the same task. Pressing the **Home** key will take you to slide 1, and pressing the **End** key will take you to the last slide). The slides do not run automatically. In order for them to do this you need to set up transitional timings (slide durations) which automatically show the next slide after a set number of seconds.

Exercise 1 Load PowerPoint and load the file saved at the end of Section 2. Create an automated presentation with slide durations shown on the design brief in Section 2 and reproduced below:

Slide no.	Slide duration (seconds)
Slide 1	5–10
Slide 2	7–15
Slide 3	15–20
Slide 4	15–25
Slide 5	15–20

METHOD
1. Click on: the ▦ **Slide Sorter** view.
2. Click on: **Slide 1** to select it.
3. Click on: the **Slide Transition** button:

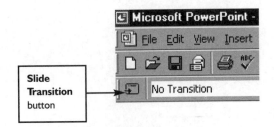

4 The Slide Transition dialogue box appears (Figure 5.22).

Figure 5.22 Slide Transition dialogue box

5 In the **Advance** section, click on: **On mouse click** so that there is no tick in the box. Click in **Automatically after** so that a tick is shown, and in the seconds box, key in the slide duration for slide 1 (in this example, it can be any number from 5 to 10).

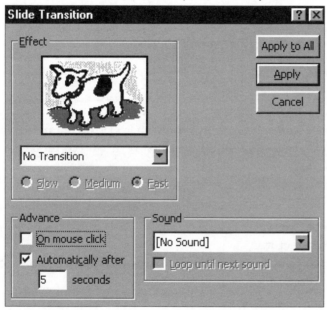

Figure 5.23 Slide Transition – 5 seconds

6 Click on: **Apply**. Slide 1 now has the duration (05) shown underneath at the left-hand side (Figure 5.24).

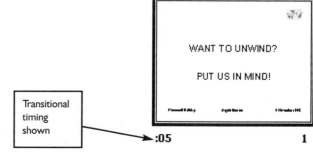

Figure 5.24 Slide 1 – duration

7 Repeat steps 2–6 for each of the other slides ensuring you have selected a timing in the range requested.
8 Save the presentation.

3.2 Running an automated presentation

 Run the automated presentation.

METHOD
1 Select slide 1 in Slide Sorter View.
2 Click on: the **Slide Show** button at the bottom left of the screen and the presentation will run automatically with the timings that have been set.

3.3 Creating transitional effects

 INFO

Transitional effects control how slides appear on the screen during a presentation. They are used to enhance the display and to ensure the audience of the presentation stay interested in it.

 Create different transition effects for each of the slides.

 INFO

House Style Sheet 2 in Section 2 gives the maximum number of transition effects for the presentation as four, and at least two different effects must be used. For practice purposes, we will look at an effect for each slide.

METHOD
1 Click on: **Slide Sorter** view.
2 Click on: **Slide 1** to select it.
3 Click on: the **down arrow** on the **Slide Transition Effects** toolbar box (Figure 5.25).

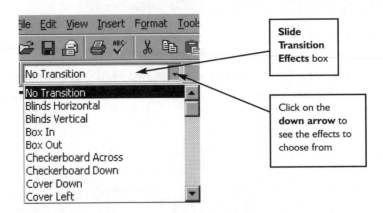

Figure 5.25 Slide Transition Effects toolbar box

4 A drop-down list appears. There are many transition effects to choose from – you can scroll down for more. Click on a transition effect – you will see a preview of the effect on slide 1. Experiment with the different effects. When you find one you like, click on that one so that it remains visible in the **Slide Transition Effects** box.

5 An icon appears beneath the slide to show it has a transition effect applied to it, as shown in Figure 5.26.

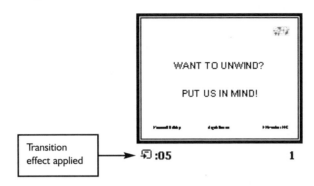

Figure 5.26 Applying a transitional effect

6 Repeat for the other slides, choosing a different transitional effect for each one.
7 Save the presentation.
8 You can now run the presentation so that you can view how the transitional effects look.

 INFO

If you want to apply the same transition effect to more than one slide in the presentation, select more than one slide by holding down the **Shift** key while selecting them. It is best not to apply too many transition effects to an automated presentation. Stick to the ones you think work the best and ensure you follow the instructions on House Style Sheet 2 when working on an IBT III assignment.

You can define the transition effect further by clicking on: the **Slide Transition** button so that the Slide Transition dialogue box appears. Here you can choose the speed of the effect and add sound. Experiment with this if you have time. (*Note:* This is not required for IBT III.)

3.4 *Creating build effects*

 INFO

Build effects determine the way text is revealed on a slide. They are usually very effective when applied to bulleted lists but can be applied to any slide object.

Exercise 4 Add different build effects to all the slides except slide 4.

 INFO

House Style Sheet 2 in Section 2 gives maximum number of build effects for the presentation as four, and at least two different effects must be used. For practice purposes, we will look at an effect for each slide except the slide with the graph.

METHOD   **1** Click on: the **Slide Sorter** View button.
          2 Click on: **Slide 1** to select it.
          3 Click on: the **down arrow** on the **Text Preset Animation** box (Figure 5.27).

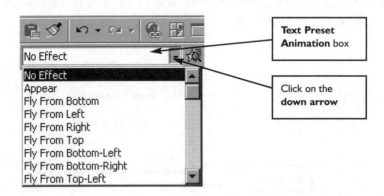

Figure 5.27   Preset Animation

4 A drop-down list appears. There are many effects to choose from – you can scroll down for more. Click on an effect. You will not see a preview, as is the case with transition effects.
5 An icon appears beneath the slide to show that a build effect has been applied to it (Figure 5.28).

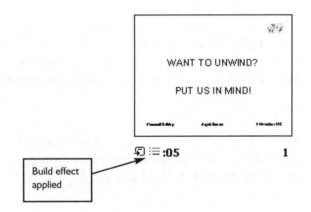

Figure 5.28   Build effect

6 To view the build effect, change to **Slide Show** View. The presentation will begin. To exit the slide show, press the **Esc** key.
7 Add build effects to the other slides as requested.
8 Save the presentation.
9 View the automated presentation.

_i_ **INFO**

The slide show can be set up to run continuously. To do this:

1 From the **Slide Show** menu, select: **Set Up Show**
2 In the **Show type** section, click on: **Loop continuously until 'Esc'**
3 Click on: **OK**.

PowerPoint quick reference for IBT III

Action	Keyboard	Mouse	Right-mouse menu	Menu
Bold text	**Ctrl + B**	Click: the **B** **Bold** button	Font	**Format**, **Font**
			Select: **Bold** from the **Font style:** menu	
Capitals (blocked)	**Caps Lock** Key in the text **Caps Lock** again to remove			Select text to be changed to capitals: **Format**, **Change Case**, **UPPERCASE**
Centre text	Select the text			
	Ctrl + E	Click: the ☰ **Center** button		**Format**, **Alignment**, **Center**
Change case	Select the text to be changed			
	From the **Format** menu, select: **Change Case** Select the appropriate case			
Close a file	**Ctrl + W**	Click: the ☒ **Close** button		**File**, **Close**
Create a new file	**Ctrl + N**	Click: the ☐ **New** button		**File**, **New**
	Select the new slide template you want to use Click: **OK**			
Cut text	Select the text to be cut			
	Ctrl + X	Click: the ✂ **Cut** button	Cut	**Edit**, **Cut**
Delete a character	Press **Delete** to delete the character to the right of the cursor Press ← (Backspace) to delete the character to the left of the cursor			
Delete a word	Double-click: the word to select it Press: **Delete**			
Delete/cut a block of text	Select the text you want to delete			
	Delete *OR* **Ctrl + X**	Click: the ✂ **Cut** button	Cut	**Edit**, **Cut**
Effects, build effects	In **Slide Sorter** View			
		Click: the ▼ down arrow next to the **Preset Animation** box	**Slide Transition** In the **Effect** section	**Slide Show**, **Slide Transition**
	Select: the effect you want from the drop-down menu			
Effects, transitional effects	In **Slide Sorter** View			
		Click: the ▼ down arrow next to the **Slide Transition Effects** box	**Slide Transition** In the **Effect** section	**Slide Show**, **Slide Transition**
	Select: the effect you want from the drop-down menu			

Action	Keyboard	Mouse	Right-mouse menu	Menu
Effects, transitional timings	In **Slide Sorter** View			
		Click: the 🖼️ **Slide Transition** button	**Slide Transition**	**Sli̲de Show**, **Slide Transition**
	In the **Advance** section Select: the timing you require			
Exit PowerPoint		Click: the ☒ **Close** button		**F̲ile**, **E̲xit**
Font	Select the text you want to change			
		Click: the ▾ down arrow next to the **Font** box Select: the font you require	**Font**	**Fo̲rmat**, **F̲ont**
			Select: the required font from the **Font:** menu	
Serif	Serif fonts have small lines at upper and lower ends of characters – eg Times New Roman			
Sans serif	Sans serif fonts do not have lines – eg Arial			
Font size	Select the text you want to change			
		Click: the ▾ down arrow next to the **Font Size** box Select: the font size you require	**Font**	**Fo̲rmat**, **F̲ont**
			Select: the required size from the **Size:** menu	
Help	**F1**			**Help̲** **Microsoft PowerPoint Help**
What's this?	**Shift + F1**			**What's T̲his?**
Importing				
graphic	From the **Insert** menu, select: **Picture**			
extract text and Excel graph	Use copy (in the source application) and paste into PowerPoint			
Insert text	Position the cursor where you want the text to appear Key in the text			
Load PowerPoint	In Windows 98 desktop			
		Double-click: the **PowerPoint** shortcut icon		**Start**, **Programs**, **Microsoft PowerPoint**
Master Slide setup				**View**, **M̲aster**, **S̲lide Master**
New Slide	**Ctrl + N**	Click: the 🖼️ **New Slide** button		**Insert**, **N̲ew Slide**
Open an existing file	**Ctrl + O**	Click: the 📂 **Open** button		**F̲ile**, **O̲pen**
	Select the appropriate directory and filename Click: **Open**			
Print – slides, thumbnails (miniatures), notes	**Ctrl + P**			**F̲ile**, **P̲rint**
	Select from the **Print what:** drop-down menu			

Action	Keyboard	Mouse	Right-mouse menu	Menu
Remove text emphasis	Select text to be changed			
	Ctrl + B (remove bold) **Ctrl + I** (remove italics) **Ctrl + U** (remove underline)	Click: the appropriate button: **B** *I* <u>U</u>	**Font**	**Format**, **Font**
				Select **Regular** from the **Font Style:** menu
Run automated presentation		Click: the 🖳 **Slide Show** button at the bottom left of the screen		**View**, **Slide Show**
Save	**Ctrl + S**	Click: the 💾 **Save** button		**File**, **Save**
	If you have not already saved the file you will be prompted to specify the directory and to name the file. If you have already done this, then Excel will automatically save it.			
Save using a different name or to a different directory				**File**, **Save As**
	Select the appropriate drive and change the filename if relevant. Click: **Save**			
Slide order	In **Slide Sorter** View Click and drag: the slide to required position			
Spell check	**F7**	Click: the 🗸 **Spelling** button		**Tools**, **Spelling**
Undo	**Ctrl + Z**	Click: the ↜ **Undo** button		**Edit**, **Undo**

Hints and tips

Check your work carefully:

Have you done everything asked? Have you:

- set up the master slide as requested?
- applied slide styles as requested?
- chosen font type (serif and sans serif) and size as specified and formatted it as requested? Does the imported text extract, graph or logo show in full? Is it the correct one?

Are text/images/lines superimposed?

Has the imported image retained its original proportions?

Have you sorted the slides as requested?

Have you applied the requested:

- build effects?
- transitional timings?
- transitional effects?

Have you printed the slides as requested?

Proofread carefully. Ensure you have not missed out exclamation marks, question marks, full stops or colons, etc where shown.

Chapter 6

Publication production using Word

1 Getting started

In this section you will learn and practise how to:
- insert an image
- import a text file
- set up document layout
- apply styles.

 INFO

In this chapter, you will be working with an existing text file and an image file (stored on the accompanying disk), together with files created in earlier sections. (The files you created earlier will have their names on your File Store Record Sheet.) Throughout the sections you will produce a publication to a set specification. This specification is found on House Style Sheet 1 – Publication page layout, and House Style Sheet 2 – Publication text style. You will need to study these carefully. In the IBT III assignment, you are able to exercise your own judgement over exact formatting of the publication. For practice purposes, this chapter will demonstrate a specific format. The Full Practice Assignment, in Part 2, will allow you to complete a similar task where you can decide on your own preferred format.

House Style Sheet 1: Publication page layout

Feature	Measurement	Position	Additional
Margins	1.5 cm left and right 2.5 cm top and bottom	–	Consistent throughout the publication
Spacing between columns	1.5 cm	–	Consistent between all columns
Page numbering	12 pt	At top of page	Not to be printed on front cover. To commence with number 2 on second page Align consistently throughout the publication
Headers/footers	12 pt	–	Footer should contain the name of the designer and the date of the publication
Pages	A4	–	Consistent orientation throughout the publication – either portrait or landscape
Columns	–	–	Two to four columns for all text except the headline Columns should be of equal size throughout the publication
Logo/image	On front cover – this should cover at least half of the width of the page When used elsewhere in the document it must be centred within the column	On front cover, centre horizontally either within margins or page. It need not be centred vertically Elsewhere, position as specified in Text For Publication (pages 101–3)	When in colour only corporate colours may be used. Black-and-white image may be used if preferred

House Style Sheet 2: Publication text style

Style name	Typeface	Point size	Feature	Alignment	Additional
Headline	Sans serif	Between 36 and 60	Bold capitals	Centre	Position horizontally across the page or margins. Must be across full width of page spanning all columns
Subheading	Sans serif	Between 18 and 22	Italic	Left	Consistent throughout the publication **Do not** apply to text included within imported graphs, images or diagrams
Body text	Serif	Between 10 and 14	–	Left	Consistent throughout the publication. Set in two to four columns
Bullet text	Serif	Use same as body text (between 10 and 14)	To include a bullet character (eg •■○)	Left	Ensure the bullet text is indented from the bullet point (hanging indent) Consistent throughout
Extract text	Sans serif	Between 10 and 14	Bold	Any	Extract style applies to *all* extracted text, except text included within graphs, images or diagrams *Do not* exceed column width Consistent throughout the publication Place a box or border around the text

1.1 Creating a front cover and inserting an image

Exercise 1 Create a front cover. This will be the first page of the four-page publication on A4-sized paper. Ensure it contains only the logo, as instructed in House Style Sheet 1.

METHOD

1 Open a new Word file. Decide what orientation to give the publication. In this example, I have chosen landscape. To do this, from the **File** menu, select: **Page Setup**, **Paper Size** tab. Ensure **Landscape** is chosen and **Apply to** whole document. Click on: **OK**.
(*Note:* Check that Paper Size A4 is chosen – it is the default.)

2 Import the image file. With the cursor at the top of the (blank) page you have just created, from the **Insert** menu, select: **Insert Picture**, **From File...** and choose the logo file to insert. Click on: **Insert**. Refer to House Style Sheet 1 for details on image positioning etc.

i **INFO**

The logo should cover at least half of the width of the page. It must be centred horizontally. It must appear in full and original proportions must be maintained. It should not be given any extra colours.

You will need to reduce the zoom so that the whole page can be seen at once. To do this change the **Zoom** on the toolbar to **Whole Page**.

Alter the size of the image (from a corner to preserve proportions) so that it covers at least half the width of the page and centre it on the page. You can check that it is centred by looking at the ruler and examining the page in Print Preview.

Save the file with a different filename.

 INFO

Saving the file with a different filename at regular intervals allows you to go back as many steps as you like if you are not happy with the result.

1.2 *Inserting a headline*

Exercise 2 On the second page, insert the headline **Naturetrail Holidays**.

METHOD   1 Insert a page break after the logo. To do this, position the cursor under the logo, from the **Insert** menu, select: **Break...**, **Page Break**. Click on: **OK**.
   2 Refer to House Style Sheet 2 for details of the heading (Headline) text.

 INFO

It should be sans serif, between 36 and 60 pt size, bold, capitals and centred. It must be positioned horizontally across the page and must span all columns. Key in the text and format it as requested.

1.3 *Importing a text file*

Exercise 3 Import the text file directly below the headline.

TEXT FOR PUBLICATION

If you are looking for a peaceful and relaxing holiday then look no further than Naturetrail Holidays. From small beginnings five years ago when the company had only one location we are now able to offer a choice of six completely different locations. Whatever your idea of the perfect place for a holiday we have the answer.

LOCATIONS

We have holiday cottages in the beautiful unspoit countryside of the Cotswolds. Here you are able to ramble along the picturesque footpaths and visit the charming villages and small towns that are dotted around this area. Our forest properties are situated in North Wales, close to Betws-y-Coed. There are endless outdoor activites in this area ranging from walking, canoeing or climing. In Cumbria you will find our lakes cottages - if you like sailing and fishing then this is the place for you. Again in North Wales, situated in the heart of Snowdonia, you will find our mountain complex. There are even trained mountaineers on hand to give you coaching in all aspects of climbing. So don't worry if you're a novice, there are activities ranging from those for beginers right through to the more experienced climber. Cornwall is the setting for our seaside properties. These are located between Boscastle and Newquay. The scenery in this area is second to none. There are wild coastal footpaths, fishing villages and sandy beaches. You will be spoilt for choice for your daily excursions! For those of you who enjoy the tranquillity of a riverside setting, you will find this at our site in Devon. Our properties are situated only 100 metres from the river Dart. Of course also in this area, in addition to riverside activities, there are beautiful moorland walks.

THE CHOICE IS YOURS. We beleve that you cannot fail to appreciate the natural beauty that abounds in all of these locations.

PROPERTIES AVAILABLE

Our properties vary in size and we have properties to suit most needs. You can choose from one to four bedrooms, with the maximum occupancy being eight people (there is the possibility that some of our properties can accommodate babies (cots and high chairs can be provided at no extra cost). Please ask the agent when booking.

PRICES

Prices vary depending on the size of the property. This year we have introduced a new system and now if you book for more than one week, any subsequent weeks are charged at a reduced rate.

The table below shows the prices relating to the different codes:

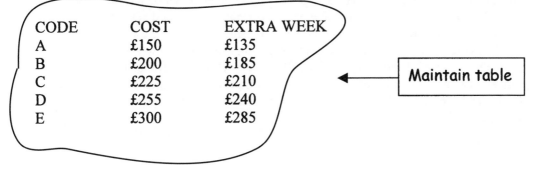

CODE	COST	EXTRA WEEK
A	£150	£135
B	£200	£185
C	£225	£210
D	£255	£240
E	£300	£285

Maintain table

Insert database report here

Why not reserve a property for our early booking period? The properties shown below are on special discount prices (deduct a further 10% from the price shown in the brochure) for this year only:

You can arrive on Friday or Saturday depending on which property you have chosen and at any time before 7 pm. Please let us know if you will be arriving later than this. Staggering arrivals in this way makes it easier to ensure that we have more staff available to give you a warm welcome. You may prefer to travel on a Friday, especially in summer when the roads are usually less congested. Whilst on the subject of transport, you will notice that most of our properties have parking adjacent to them. Where this is not the case your vehicle may be left in the parking areas which are never more than 50 metres away. For unloading purposes, parking outside the property is perfectly acceptable but please remember to move your vehicle as soon as you can since it will cause an obstruction.

Your property will have been fully cleaned and inspected beffore your arrival which can be anytime after 12 noon. All bed linen is provided but you will need to bring your own towels. All properties are self-catering but to help you settle in, we do provide a small grocery basket containing essentials, such as bread and milk. Should you find that things are not to your liking, please contact us straight away. WE PRIDE OURSELVES ON GIVING YOU THE BEST SERVICE AT ALL TIMES.

Insert logo here

LOYALTY SAVINGS

Naturetrail Holidays are pleased to to announce an important bonus for customers who have taken holidays with us in the past. We are now able to give substantial discounts on your holiday booking this year.

If you book your holiday before the end of January you will be entitled to a 20% discount on the standard cost of your chosen property (subject to its availability). If you book before the end of March you will be entitled to a 10% discount on the standard cost.

We feel that this is a very generous ofer and hope that you will be able to make your bookings early to benefit from the maximum savings.

Each 'loyalty' customer will be entered into our prize draw. We will be offering cash prizes ranging from £50 to £500 to those lucky ones picked out at random. If you are eligible for this discount, please have your previous booking reference to hand when you call. If you no longer have your booking reference, don't worry we will be able to look up your details on our database.

HOW TO BOOK

Insert spreadsheet report here

Our properties can be booked from our Head Office by telephoning 01234 29786. We are open from 7 am to 7 pm every day except Sunday. Our regional offices can also help you with any queries that you may have. They are each allocated several properties that are their major concern. Choosing the right accomodation to suit your needs can be difficult and we want to help you make an informed choice. You can rely on our staff giving informative and friendly advice. Our computerised booking system gives instant availability of our properties so that we can suggest an alternative should your first choice be taken. Shown below are the properties dealt with by our Bristol office:

As you can see each regional office deals with properties from all of the locations. Our staff training ensures that all staff have visited the six locations and are aware of the differences between them.

When booking please ensure that you have the following details to hand:

Bullet text

⌐ Reference of Property
Price Code
Date Required
Number in Party
Vehicle Registration Number
Credit Card Number
└ Former Booking Ref (if applicable)

Here at Naturetrail Holidays we pride ourselves in providing an excelent booking service and we hope that you feel that this level of excellence carries through to all of our operations. We know how important it is that everything runs smoothly so that you are able to relax and enjoy yourselves.

So what are you waiting for? Have another look through our brochure and imagiine the fun that you'll have with Naturetrail Holidays.

DON'T DELAY - BOOK TODAY.

METHOD

1 Position the cursor where you want the start of the text to appear.
2 From the **Insert** menu, select: **File....** Choose the file location and name.
3 Click on: **OK**.

1.4 Spellchecking

Exercise 4 Perform a spellcheck and resave the file.

1.5 Setting margins

Exercise 5 Set the margins as specified.

METHOD

1 Press: **Ctrl + Home** to take the cursor to the beginning of the file.
2 From the **File** menu, select: **Page Setup**. Select the **Margins** tab and set the margins as requested on House Style Sheet 1.

i **INFO**

Margins should be 1.5 cm left and right, 2.5 cm top and bottom.

3 Ensure **Whole document** is selected in the **Apply to** section.

1.6   *Setting styles and alignment*

Exercise 6   Change the font typeface, point size and enhancement of the subheadings, body text and bullet text to those requested on House Style Sheet 2. Align the text as specified.

METHOD   1   Examine House Style Sheet 2 to determine the text style.
           2   Select the text in turn and format, align and enhance it as requested.

           Save your work.

INFO

Instead of using the manual method of changing text styles, the following method can be used.

METHOD   1   Apply the appropriate formatting to text that has been keyed in.
           2   Select the text.
           3   From the **Format** menu, select: **Style**.
           4   The Style dialogue box appears. Click on: **New** (Figure 6.1).

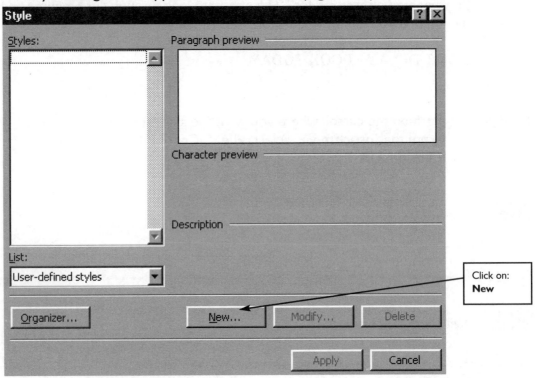

Figure 6.1 Style dialogue box

           5   The New Style dialogue box appears (Figure 6.2).

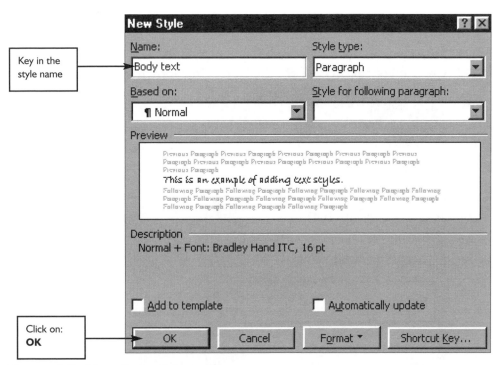

Figure 6.2 New Style dialogue box

6 In the **Name** box, key in the style name, eg Body text, Headline.
  Note: A description of the text style is shown in the Description section.
7 Click on: **OK**.
8 You are returned to the Style dialogue box. The style you have chosen is now shown. Click on: **Apply** (Figure 6.3).

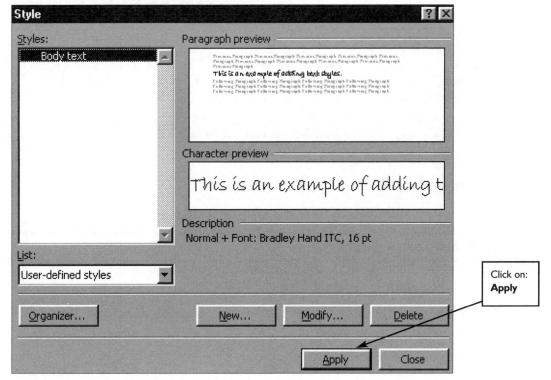

Figure 6.3 Applying a style

9 Repeat the above for each style of text you require.

To apply the text style to a block of text:

1 Select the text you want to apply the style to.
2 Choose the text style from the **Style** drop-down list (Figure 6.4).

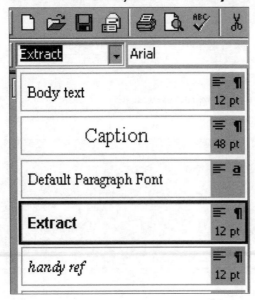

Figure 6.4 Style drop-down list

 INFO

When carrying out IBT III assignments, you may want to change the style to ensure good layout. To amend a text style:

1 Format the text as required.
2 Select the text.
3 Click on: the **down arrow** so that the Style drop-down list is showing.
4 Click on: the style you want to amend. The Modify Style box appears.
5 Click to **Update** the style to reflect recent changes.
6 Click on: **OK**.

1.7 *Page numbering*

 Number the pages as specified.

METHOD 1 Position the cursor at the start of the document (**Ctrl + Home**).
2 Refer to House Style Sheet 1.

 INFO

Page numbers should be at top of page, 12 point size, not printed on front cover. To commence with number 2 on second page. Aligned consistently throughout the publication.

3 From the **Insert** menu, select: **Page Numbers...**; the Page Numbers dialogue box appears. Choose the **Position** for page numbers, choose the **Alignment** for page numbers and ensure that **Show number on first page** is not selected. Click on: **OK** (Figure 6.5).

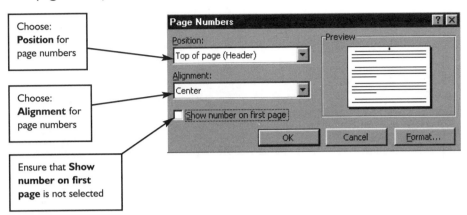

Choose: **Position** for page numbers

Choose: **Alignment** for page numbers

Ensure that **Show number on first page** is not selected

Figure 6.5 Page Numbers dialogue box

4 To set the point size for the page numbers, double-click on any page number. The **Header and Footer** dialogue box appears. Click once on the page number and then drag the mouse over it to select it. Change the font size using the drop-down Font Size list.
5 Click on: **Close**.

 INFO

Use the **Format** option in the **Page Numbers** dialogue box if further formatting is

1.8 *Setting up columns*

 Set up columns as requested on House Style Sheet 1.

Exercise 8

INFO

You can decide how many columns to have across the page (between two and four). In this instance I will choose three. When completing the Full Practice Assignment in Part 2, experiment with a different number of columns.

METHOD
1 Select the text that needs to be put into columns.
2 From the **Format** menu, select: **Columns...**; the Columns dialogue box appears (Figure 6.6).

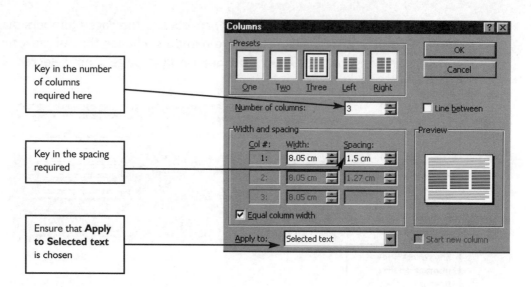

Key in the number of columns required here

Key in the spacing required

Ensure that **Apply to Selected text** is chosen

Figure 6.6 Columns dialogue box

3 Change the number of columns to 3 and the spacing to 1.5 cm. Ensure that **Apply to Selected text** is chosen.
Note: The columns will not show in Normal View. Switch to Print Layout view to see what the columns look like.

1.9 *Adding bullets*

Exercise 9 Add bullets to the list where requested.

METHOD   1 Select the list.
  2 Click on: the **Bullet** button.
   Note: The list may be divided between two columns. This can be altered later.

 INFO

You can choose different styles of bullets. Select the bulleted list. From the **Format** menu, select: **Bullets and Numbering**... Select the bullet style and click on: **OK**.

1.10 *Adding headers and footers*

Exercise 10 Add a header/footer as requested.

METHOD   1 Move the cursor to the start of the document (**Ctrl + Home**).
  2 Refer to House Style Sheet 1 for details.

 INFO

The footer should contain the name of the designer and the date of publication. Font size 12 point.

3 From the **View** menu, select: **Header and Footer**. The Header and Footer dialogue box appears (Figure 6.7).

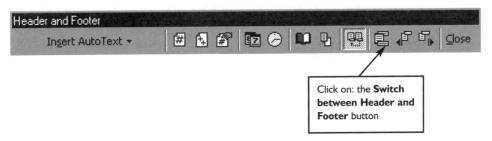

Click on: the **Switch between Header and Footer** button

Figure 6.7 Header and Footer box

4 Click on: the **Switch between Header and Footer** button. The Footer section appears (Figure 6.8).

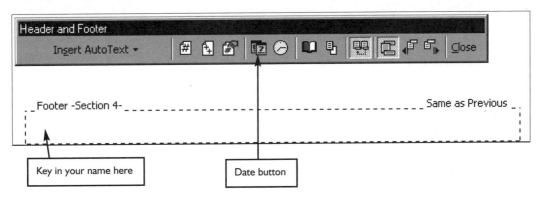

Key in your name here

Date button

Figure 6.8 Footer section

5 Key in your name directly into the Footer section.
6 Press the **tab** key (or **spacebar**) several times to move the cursor across the page.
7 Click on the date toolbar button (see Figure 6.8) to insert today's date.
8 Select all the text in the footer and change the point size as requested on House Style Sheet 1.

INFO

Check the date is correct. The date may not be set up correctly on your computer. If it shows the wrong date, highlight it to select it, then press the **Delete** key. Key in the date.

Save your file.

2 Adding extract text and borders, inserting from other applications, publication layout, printing

In this section you will learn and practise how to:
■ add extract text
■ add borders
■ insert a database report
■ insert a spreadsheet report
■ insert an image within the body of the document
■ select optimum layout for the publication
■ print your publication.

2.1 Adding extract text

Exercise 1 Insert the following extract text at the end of the document you created in the last section. It begins:

We will be continuing...

and ends with:

...you may win one of ten super cash prizes.

This extract is the first sentence of the last paragraph in a Word file (which can be found on the accompanying disk). The file has the heading LOYALTY SAVINGS. Format the text as specified on House Style Sheet 2.

METHOD 1 Load the Word file created in Section 1. Position the cursor where you want the text to appear.
2 Open the Word file containing the extract text.
3 Select the text to be inserted. Click on: the **Copy** button.
4 Close the Word file.
5 Click on: the **Paste** button. The text is pasted into the publication.
6 Format and align the extract text as specified.

2.2 Adding borders

Exercise 2 Add a border around the extract text.

METHOD 1 Select the text.
2 From the **Format** menu, select: **Borders and Shading.** The Borders and Shading dialogue box appears (Figure 6.9).

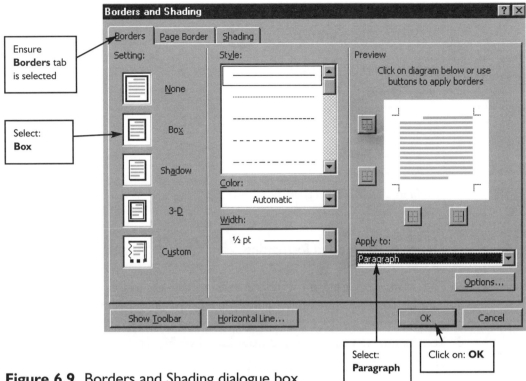

Ensure **Borders** tab is selected

Select: **Box**

Select: **Paragraph**

Click on: **OK**

Figure 6.9 Borders and Shading dialogue box

3 Ensure the **Borders** tab is selected.
4 From the **Setting** section, select: **Box**.
5 In the **Apply to** section, select: **Paragraph**.
6 Click on: **OK**.
Note: You can shade the box by clicking on the **Shading** tab and making selections.

2.3 Inserting a database report

Exercise 3 Insert the database report, saved in Chapter 3, Section 2, Exercise 4 where shown. (You should have entered details of this on your File Store Record Sheet.)

METHOD
1 Position the cursor where the database report is to appear.
2 Open the file containing the database report and select the report text.
3 Click on: the **Copy** button and close the file containing the database report.
4 Click on: the **Paste** button.

i **INFO**

If the formatting does not carry across exactly, it may appear something like this:

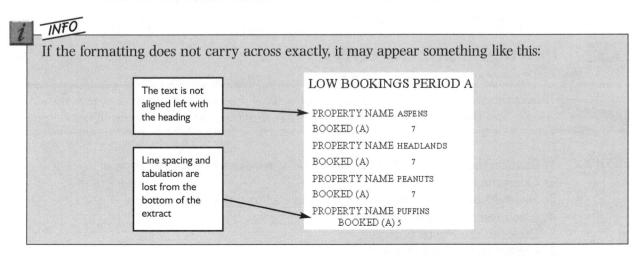

The text is not aligned left with the heading

Line spacing and tabulation are lost from the bottom of the extract

LOW BOOKINGS PERIOD A

PROPERTY NAME ASPENS
BOOKED (A)   7
PROPERTY NAME HEADLANDS
BOOKED (A)   7
PROPERTY NAME PEANUTS
BOOKED (A)   7
PROPERTY NAME PUFFINS
        BOOKED (A) 5

5 Click on: the **Show/Hide** button to see the hidden formatting (Figure 6.10).

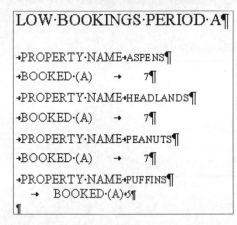

Figure 6.10 Hidden formatting

6 To line up text: delete the characters on the left in front of the words.
7 The bottom two lines have different line spacing. Select them, then from the **Format** menu, select: **Paragraph**. Set the **Line Spacing** to 1.5. Click on: **OK**.
8 Your database report should now look like Figure 6.11.

Figure 6.11 Corrected database report

9 To correct the alignment of the 5 in the last line:

a Select all except the title of the report.
b On the ruler drag the **Left** tab marker so that it is in line with the numbers.
c Deselect the text by clicking in a white space.

10 Click on: the **Show/Hide** toolbar button to turn Show off.
11 Format the extract as specified.

2.4 Inserting a spreadsheet report

Exercise 4   Insert the spreadsheet report, saved in Chapter 4, Section 3, Exercise 5 where shown. (*Note:* You should have entered details of this on your File Store Record Sheet.)

METHOD
1 Position the cursor where you want the spreadsheet report to appear.
2 Open the spreadsheet report.
3 Highlight the extract to be inserted and click on: the **Copy** button.
4 Close the spreadsheet file.
5 Click on: the **Paste** button.
6 Format the extract as specified.

2.5   *Inserting the image within the document*

 Insert the logo image where specified.

 INFO

Since you already have this image on the front cover of the publication, this is simply a matter of copying and pasting it to the requested place. You will need to resize and position it as specified on House Style Sheet 1.

2.6   *Selecting optimum layout for the publication*

 Tidy up the publication so that it is copyfitted as follows:

- ■ Headings/subheadings must not be split from the related text.
- ■ Line spacing between subheadings, paragraphs and imported data must be applied consistently.
- ■ One line or less of text is grouped with the rest of related text ('widows and orphans').
- ■ No more than two clear lines of white space are left at the end of columns throughout the document, the only exception being at the end of the publication.
- ■ Text and imported data are adjusted so that they are not superimposed on other text or data.
- ■ Imported data must not be split across columns or pages.

INFO

There is no one optimum way to achieve the above. This will vary depending on what attributes you have chosen. It is important to save your work before commencing on this exercise so that you have access to your original file should things go wrong. You will need to experiment until you are sure all the points above have been addressed and incorporated.

2.7   *Printing your publication*

Print your publication.

METHOD
  1   Check to see how the document looks using **Print Preview**.
  2   Carry out any further adjustments.
  3   Perform a final spellcheck in case any words have gone awry.
  4   Print and proofread the printout carefully checking that it matches the House Style Sheets and conforms to the conditions set out in the previous exercise.

3 Using drawing features

In this section you will learn and practise how to:
■ use drawing features
  – lines
  – circles
  – boxes
  – ellipses
  – fill/pattern.

 INFO

You may be asked to use the drawing features of Word in the publication assignment. Only use them if requested. They are easy to use and also useful to know so that you can enhance any of your Word documents you work on outside IBT III work.

 Exercise 1   Create a new Word document and add drawing features to it.

METHOD With a new Word document open, ensure the Drawing toolbar is visible. If not, from the **View** menu, select: **Toolbars**, click on: **Drawing** so that a tick appears next to it.

The Drawing toolbar buttons used in this section are shown in Figure 6.12.

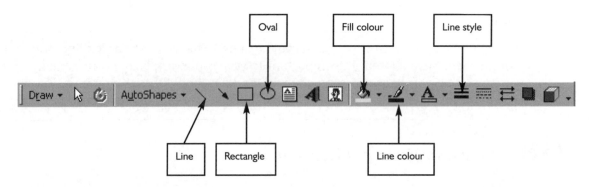

Figure 6.12 Drawing toolbar buttons

Adding a line
  1 Click on: the **Line** toolbar button.
  2 Position the crosshair where you want the line to start.
  3 Hold down the left mouse button and drag the mouse to where you want the line to end. Release the mouse button.

Formatting the line
  1 Select the line by clicking on it. When it is selected, handles appear at each end.
  2 Click on: the **Line Style** toolbar button.
  3 Click on: the line style you want.

Adding a circle or ellipse

1 Click on: the **Oval** button.
2 Hold down the left mouse button and drag out to the required shape.
3 Release the mouse button.

Adding a box

Follow the method for a circle/ellipse, shown above.

Filling a shape with colour

1 Select the shape to fill.
2 Click on: the **down arrow** next to the **Fill Color** button.
3 Click on: the chosen colour.

Filling a shape with a pattern

Follow steps 1 and 2 above.

1 Click on: **Fill Effects**. The Fill Effects dialogue box appears.
2 Click on: the **Pattern** tab.
3 Click on: the chosen pattern. Click on: **OK**.

INFO

Experiment with the other Drawing buttons to create some stunning effects.

Word quick reference for IBT III

Action	Keyboard	Mouse	Right-mouse menu	Menu
Bold text	Select text to embolden			
	Ctrl + B	Click: the **B** **Bold** button	**Font**	**Format, Font**
			Select: **Bold** from the **Font style:** menu	
Borders				**Format, Borders and Shading**
	Select the border options you require			
Capitals (blocked)	**Caps Lock** Key in the text **Caps Lock** again to remove			Select text to be changed to capitals: **Format, Change Case, UPPERCASE**
Centre text	Select the text			
	Ctrl + E	Click: the ≡ **Center** button	**Paragraph**	**Format, Paragraph**
			Select **Centered** from the **Alignment:** drop-down menu	
Change case	Select the text to be changed From the **Format** menu, select: **Change Case** Select the appropriate case			
Close a file	**Ctrl + W**	Click: the ☒ **Close** button		**File, Close**
Columns		Click: the ▦ **Columns** button and drag the mouse until you have selected the number of columns		**Format, Columns** Select the number of columns and options you require
Create a new file	**Ctrl + N**	Click: the ☐ **New** button		**File, New**
Cut text	Select the text to be cut			
	Ctrl + X	Click: the ✂ **Cut** button	**Cut**	**Edit, Cut**
Delete a character	Press **Delete** to delete the character to the right of the cursor Press ← (Backspace) to delete the character to the left of the cursor			
Delete a word	Double-click: the word to select it Press: **Delete**			
Delete/cut a block of text	Select the text you want to delete			
	Delete OR **Ctrl + X**	Click: the ✂ **Cut** button	**Cut**	**Edit, Cut**
Drawing features	To display the **Drawing** toolbar: From the **View** menu, select: **Toolbars, Drawing**			
	Select from the toolbar buttons (see Chapter 6, Section 3)			

Action	Keyboard	Mouse	Right-mouse menu	Menu
Exit Word		Click: the ☒ **Close** button		**F**ile, E**x**it
Font	Select the text you want to change			
		Click: the ▾ down arrow next to the **Font** box Select: the font you require	**Font** Select: the required font from the **Font:** menu	F**o**rmat, **F**ont
Font size	Select the text you want to change			
		Click: the ▾ down arrow next to the **Font Size** box Select: the font size you require	**Font** Select: the required size from the **Size:** menu	F**o**rmat, **F**ont
Headers and Footers				**V**iew, **H**eader and Footer
Help	**F1**			**Help** **Microsoft Word Help**
What's this?	**Shift + F1**			**What's This?**
Indenting		Click: the ⬛ **Increase Indent** button Click: the ⬛ **Decrease Indent** button	**Paragraph** In the **Indentation** section, select your options as appropriate	F**o**rmat, **P**aragraph
To remove indent				
Insert text	Position the cursor where you want the text to appear Key in the text			
Justified margins	Select the text you want to change			
	Ctrl + J	Click: the ⬛ **Justify** button	**Paragraph** Select **Justified** from the **Alignment** drop-down menu	F**o**rmat, **P**aragraph
Line length, changing		Use the ruler (see separate table)		**F**ile, **P**age Set**u**p, **Margins** (see separate table)
Line spacing			**Paragraph** In the **Spacing** section, select the options you require	F**o**rmat, **P**aragraph, **Indents and Spacing**
Load Word	In Windows 98 desktop			
		Double-click: the **Word** shortcut icon		**Start, Programs, Microsoft Word**
Margins				**F**ile, **P**age Set**u**p, **Margins**

Action	Keyboard	Mouse	Right-mouse menu	Menu
Move a block of text	Select: the text to be moved Cut it and paste it where you want it moved to *OR* Select: the text to be moved Click and drag: it to the correct position Release the mouse button			
Moving around the document	Use the cursor keys (see separate table for more)	Click: in the required position		
Open an existing file	**Ctrl + O**	Click: the 📂 **Open** button		**File**, **Open**
	Select the appropriate directory and filename Click: **Open**			
Page break, adding	**Ctrl + Enter**			**Insert**, **Break**, **Page Break**, **OK**
Page break, deleting	Place the cursor on the page break Press: **Delete**			
Page numbering				**Insert**, **Page Numbers** Select the required options
Page Setup				**File**, **Page Setup** (Choose from **Margins**, **Paper size**, **Paper source**, **Layout**)
Paper size	(See Page Setup)			
Paragraphs - splitting/joining	*Splitting:* Move the cursor to the first letter of the new paragraph Press: **Enter** twice *Joining:* Move the cursor to the first character of the second paragraph Press ← (Backspace) twice (Press the spacebar to insert a space after a full stop)			
Print file	**Ctrl + P** Select the options you need Press: **Enter**	Click: the 🖨 **Print** button		**File**, **Print** Select the options you need and click **OK**
Print preview		Click: the 🔍 **Print Preview** button		**File**, **Print Preview**
Ragged right margin	Select text			
	Ctrl + L	Click: the ▤ **Align Left** button	**Paragraph**	**Format**, **Paragraph**
			Select **Left** from the **Alignment:** drop-down menu	

Action	Keyboard	Mouse	Right-mouse menu	Menu
Remove text emphasis	Select text to be changed			
	Ctrl + B (remove bold) **Ctrl + I** (remove italics) **Ctrl + U** (remove underline)	Click: the appropriate button: **B** *I* U	**Font**	**Format**, **Font** Select **Regular** from the **Font Style:** menu
Replace text	**Ctrl + H**			**Edit**, **Replace**
Save	**Ctrl + S**	Click: the 💾 **Save** button		**File**, **Save**
	If you have not already saved the file you will be prompted to specify the directory and to name the file. If you have already done this, then Word will automatically save it.			
Save using a different name or to a different directory				**File**, **Save As**
	Select the appropriate drive and change the filename if relevant. Click: **Save**			
Spellcheck	**F7**	Click: the ✓ **Spelling** button		**Tools**, **Spelling and Grammar**
Styles	Select the text, from the **Format** menu, select **Style**			
Tables		Click: the ▦ **Insert Table** button		**Table**, **Insert**, **Table**
	(See separate information below)			
Tabs	(See separate information below)			
Undo	**Ctrl + Z**	Click: the ↺ **Undo** button		**Edit**, **Undo**
Widows and Orphans				**Format**, **Paragraph**, **Line and Page Breaks** Select: **Widow/Orphan control**

Moving around the document

Move	Keyboard action
To top of document	**Ctrl + Home**
To end of document	**Ctrl + End**
Left word by word	**Ctrl + ←**
Right word by word	**Ctrl + →**
To end of line	**End**
To start of line	**Home**

Selecting text

Selecting what	Action
Whole document	**Ctrl + A**
One word	Double-click on the word
One paragraph	Double-click in the selection border
Any block of text	Click at the start of the text; press: **Shift**; click at the end of the text
Deselect text	Click in any white space

(*Note*: See appendix for keyboard shortcuts.)

Line lengths

Line lengths	Margin width
12,7 cm (5 in)	4.15 cm (1.63 in)
14 cm ($5\frac{1}{2}$ in)	3.5 cm (1.38 in)
15.3 cm (6 in)	2.85 cm (1.13 in)
16.5 cm ($6\frac{1}{2}$ in)	2.25 cm (0.88 in)

Indentation using the ruler

Select the text you want to indent.

Drag the respective markers (Figure 6.13) on the ruler to the location you want

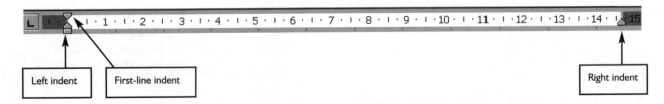

Figure 6.13 Ruler markers

First-line indents and hanging paragraphs using the Format menu

1   Select the text.
2   From the **Format** menu, select: **Paragraph**.
3   In the Paragraph dialog box, ensure the **Indents and Spacing** tab is selected.
4   In the Special box, click on the down arrow and select **Hanging** or **First line**, as appropriate.
5   Check the Preview box (Figure 6.14) to see what the text will look like.
6   Click on: **OK**.

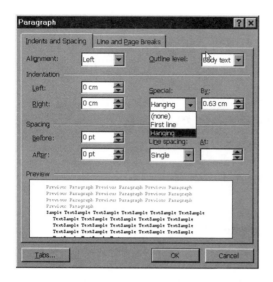

Figure 6.14 Paragraph Preview box

Working with tables

Inserting rows/columns: Select the row below where you want to insert new rows, or select the column to the right of where you want to insert new columns. Click the right mouse over the selection. From the pop-up menu, select: **Insert Rows** or **Insert Columns**.

Adding a row at the end of a table: Click in the last cell of the last row, and press the **Tab** key.

Adding a column to the right of the last column in a table: Click just outside the right-hand column. From the **Table** menu, select: **Select**, **Column**, Right-click on the selection. Select **Insert Columns**.

Deleting a table and its contents: Select the table by clicking anywhere in it. From the **Table** menu, select: **Select**, **Table**. Click on: the **Cut** button.

Deleting cells, rows or columns from a table: Select the cells, rows, or columns you want to delete. Right-click on the selection and select: **Delete Cells**.

Ensuring the contents fit the cells: Select the table (position the cursor in the table; from the **Table** menu, select: **Select**, **Table**.) From the **Table** menu, select: **AutoFit** *or* select the column/row border to change and drag the column/row border to the required position.

Working with tabs

Tabs are used to line up columns and Word offers four types of tab.

By default, tabs are set every 1.27 cm ($\frac{1}{2}$ in) from the left margin. When a new tab is set, Word clears any default tabs set to the left of the new tab stop. The type of tab stop can be chosen by clicking on the tab button at the left-hand edge of the ruler (Figure 6.15).

Common tabs include:

L   Left tab

⌐   Right tab

⊥   Centre tab

⊥·   Decimal tab

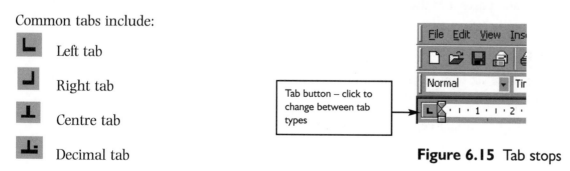

Figure 6.15 Tab stops

Hard spaces

It is better not to split some words at line ends eg Mr Brown – Mr and Brown should be on the same line. A hard space keeps the words on either side of it together. To insert a hard space: Instead of just pressing the spacebar between the words, press **Ctrl + Shift + Spacebar**.

Importing information using copy and paste method

1 Load the Word file.
2 Position the cursor where you want the import to appear.
3 Load the program that contains the import... **Start** button, **Programs**.
4 Load the file that contains the data to import.
5 Select the data that you want to copy.
6 Click on: the **Copy** button in the application with the selected data.
7 Click on: **Microsoft Word** file on the taskbar.
8 Click on: the **Paste** button.
9 Close the application you have pasted from by clicking the right mouse over the application file button on the taskbar, and clicking **Close**. (Do not save changes.)
10 Resize as necessary.

Using Office Links and importing using the Insert menu

You can also transfer data between applications using Office Links (you can import reports using this but you will still have to cut and paste into the Word document). You can import by selecting **Object** from the **Insert** menu. Check the **Help** menu for **Linked Objects and Importing Data** for more information.

An example of how to import an Access report into Word follows:

METHOD   1 Move the cursor to where the database extract is to be inserted.
2 With Word still loaded, load Access and open the database file.
3 Open the report that you want to import.
4 Click on: the **down arrow** of the **OfficeLinks** button.
5 Click on: **Publish It with MS Word** (Figure 6.16).

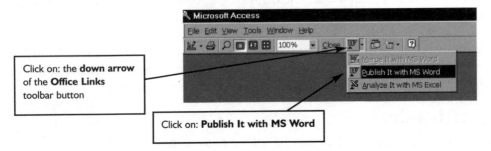

Figure 6.16 Office Links

6 The report will appear on screen as a Word document.
7 Copy and paste it in the normal way.

Hints and tips

Close down applications as soon as you have finished with them to ensure your computer is not slowed down unnecessarily.

Check spacing after importing. Keep it consistent throughout.

Common errors made when completing IBT III assignments:

■ Not proofreading well enough – missing out words or longer portions of text.

■ Inconsistency of spacing – between words, between paragraphs.

Have you carried out all the instructions?

Have you conformed to the House Style Sheets? Check carefully.

PART 2

Full Practice Assignment

Introduction

This part contains an example full practice assignment as it is presented for IBT III. All the skills have been covered in Part 1 and some of the exercises are repeated here for you to consolidate those skills. The assignment differs in places from that given in Part 1 resulting in the printouts varying in subtle ways. This allows you to approach this assignment without necessarily knowing exactly what to expect, making it much more worthwhile.

Study the format of the assignment in detail before you begin. You will soon notice the integrated approach of assignments at this level. Make notes before you begin and keep track of each piece of work as you go through by ticking off those tasks that you have completed. This will enable you to ensure that nothing is left out.

Read all the instructions very carefully so that you fully understand what you need to do and always check your work thoroughly at every stage.

The assignment consists of:

- a scenario
- Section A – File Management and E-mail
- Section B – Database
- Section C – Spreadsheet
- Section D – Presentation
- Section E – E-mail
- Section F – Publication

Source Documentation booklets are included within the set of material:

- Correspondence File
- Design Brief – Presentation
- Design Brief – Publication

A File Store Record Sheet should be completed throughout and a Time Log Sheet is included (in the appendix) and should also be completed. A total of 10 hours is allowed to complete the assignment.

Scenario

You work for a company called 'Naturetrail Holidays'. This organisation has properties for rent during the spring and summer months. The annual presentation to Regional Offices is about to take place.

The Publicity Officer will be doing the presentation and will need help in preparing materials that will be presented to the regional office staff. You have been asked to help by extracting information stored in the database and spreadsheet files and include this information in a publication and an automated presentation.

The publication will consist of a four-page leaflet (which will be used in conjunction with our brochure). The automated presentation will be on display in the foyer from the presentation day onwards.

You will need to access files from the accompanying disk in order to carry out some of the assignments. *So that you always have access to the original files, it is **essential** to make a copy of the disk before starting on any of the exercises.*

Note: During an actual assignment the scenario files are e-mailed to you.

To complete the project you will carry out the following tasks:

a)	**Process source data**	You will examine and update a database, which contains information of all the company's properties.
		You will examine and update a spreadsheet, which contains details of the holiday properties for rental. Use functions and formulae to complete the spreadsheet.
		Data Request Forms are used to detail the data required for the project.
b)	**File management**	You will create directories/folders and subdirectories/folders to contain the files used throughout the project. In addition you will be required to name, save and record details of new and amended files and ensure that copies are made for back-up purposes.
c)	**Communications**	You will access an e-mail message, retrieve files sent electronically and respond on completion of the project, by sending your own message with an automated presentation as an attached file.
d)	**Presentation**	You will be given a Design Brief to produce an automated promotional presentation incorporating text, an image and a graph.
e)	**Publication**	You will be given a Design Brief incorporating text, an image and extracted information.

During the **Source Data Processing** section of the assignment you will be required to produce a number of printouts. You will submit these to the Publicity Officer (Tutor/Local Assessor) to be checked. Although you are ultimately responsible for the accuracy of the work, the Publicity Officer may point out errors that need to be corrected.

You will also be required to produce a number of printouts for the **Presentation** and **Publication** sections of the assignments. Once these have been submitted to the Tutor/Local assessor no amendments are allowed.

Project

Assignment Section A – File Management and E-mail

On commencement of the project you will be sent a number of source files via e-mail, to enable you to carry out specified tasks. You are required to create directories/folders and sub-directories/subfolders for the storage and retrieval both of these files and the files you produce.

You will also be supplied with a hard copy of the Correspondence File, which is referred to in Section 3 of the project.

1   (a)   Create a directory/folder for the project.

      (b)   Record the directory/folder name on your File Store Record Sheet.

      (c)   Within this directory/folder create and name two sub-directories/subfolders:

- one is for working copies

- one is for copy files.

      (d)   Record the names on your File Store Record Sheet.

2   You have been sent an e-mail message (these files are stored on disk):

      (a)   Open your mailbox and access this message.

      (b)   Follow the instructions contained in the e-mail message.

      (c)   Print a copy, including transaction details.

Assignment Section B – Database

Access the database containing details of holiday properties offered by the company.

3   Refer to the memos in your Correspondence File (Source Documentation) and carry out all the specified amendments to the database.

4   Ensure the updated database has been saved in the sub-directory/folder created for the working files. Use your File Store Record Sheet to record the full details, including the name of the sub-directory/folder.

5   Refer to the Data Request Forms in your Correspondence File (Source Documentation) which detail the information required from the database:

    (a)   Save the queries and reports using unique names.

           Use your File Store Record Sheet to record the full details including the name of the sub-directory/folder. **Indicate which of the reports created will be used later in the publication.**

    (b)   Print the queries in table format, including the field headings. Ensure all data is displayed in full.

    (c)   Print the reports including the report title and field headings. Ensure all the data is displayed in full.

    Submit these printouts to your Supervisor.

Assignment Section C – Spreadsheet

Access the spreadsheet containing an analysis of property income for 1999.

6   Refer to the memos in your Correspondence File (Source Documentation) and carry out all the specified amendments to the spreadsheet.

7   Using a unique filename – save the amended spreadsheet in the sub-directory/folder created for all the working files. Use your File Store Record Sheet to record the full details including the name of the sub-directory/folder.

8   (a)   Print the entire spreadsheet. Ensure all the data is displayed in full.

     (b)   Change the display to show the formulae. Print the entire spreadsheet ensuring that the formulae are displayed in full.

9   (a)   In the Property Details section, hide only the 3 columns containing the following headings:

     - BOOKED(A)

     - BOOKED(B)

     - PRICE CODE

     (b)   Change the display to show values.

     (c)   Produce a printout of the PROPERTY DETAILS section only, displaying only those columns still visible. Ensure all the headings and data are displayed in full.

10   Submit these printouts to your Supervisor to check the data is correct.

11   After printing, change the spreadsheet to display the previously hidden columns.

12   In your Correspondence File (Source Documentation) refer to the Data Request Forms which detail the information required from the spreadsheet.

13   (a)   Using a unique file reference – save the spreadsheet extract in the sub-directory/folder created for working files.

     Use your File Store Record Sheet to record the full details including the name of the sub-directory/folder. **Indicate which extract and graph will be used later in the project, as specified in the Data Request Forms.**

     (b)   Produce the printouts as specified in the Data Request Forms.

14   Submit this printout to your Supervisor.

Do not proceed until authorised to do so.

Assignment Section D – Presentation

Do not begin this section until your Supervisor has authorised you to do so.

Delete all database and spreadsheet files **not** listed on your File Store Record Sheet from the working files sub-directory/folder.

15   Create an automated presentation to be used at the annual meeting for regional offices. Consult your Presentation Design Brief – (Source Documentation) for details and layout required for the regional presentation.

16   Access the supplied image and the text file used in a recent promotion. Extract the text to be included in the presentation.

17   Details for the positioning of the extracts are provided in the Presentation Design Brief – (Source Documentation). Refer to your File Store Record Sheet for the filename of the graph to be included in the presentation.

18   Run the presentation to check it meets all requirements.

19   (a)   Using a unique filename, save the presentation in a format enabling it to be run at a later date.

       (b)   This file should be saved in the sub-directory/folder created for all the working files.

       (c)   Use your File Store Record Sheet to record the full details including the name of the sub-directory/folder.

20   Print one copy of each slide **and** an overview on one page containing a miniature (thumbnail) of each slide.

21   (a)   It has been decided to change the order of the slides. Please move Slide 1 to become the last slide in the presentation.

       (b)   Print a copy as an overview on one page containing a miniature (thumbnail) of each slide.

       (c)   Re-save the amended presentation retaining the existing filename.

22   (a)   Copy the presentation file you have saved to the sub-directory/folder created for copies.

       (b)   Use your File Store Record Sheet to record the full details, including the name of the sub-directory/folder.

Assignment Section E – E-mail

23 Send an e-mail message confirming you have finished the presentation and are sending the presentation file for viewing.

Attach the presentation file to your e-mail message.

Address this message to your Supervisor and to one other person specified by your Supervisor.

Ensure your name is included as a reference.

24 Print a copy of your e-mail message, including transaction details.

Assignment Section F – Publication

Produce a publication containing information to be used in the NatureTrail catalogue. The publication will consist of supplied text, the NatureTrail logo and extracts taken from the database and spreadsheet.

25   Use the supplied text and image files.

26   Consult your File Store Record Sheet for the filenames of the database and spreadsheet extracts to be included in the publication.

27   Consult your Publication Design Brief – (Source Documentation), for details of the layout required.

28   Review your document to ensure it is complete and perform a spellcheck, correcting any errors found.

29   (a)   Using a unique filename, save the publication in the sub-directory/folder created for working files.

    (b)   Use your File Store Record Sheet to record the full details, including the name of the sub-directory/folder.

30   Print the entire promotional publication on A4 paper.

31   (a)   Copy the publication file you have saved to the sub-directory/folder created for copies.

    (b)   Use your File Store Record Sheet to record the details, including the name of the sub-directory/folder.

SOURCE DOCUMENTATION

CORRESPONDENCE FILE

MEMORANDUM

TO: ALL REGIONAL AGENTS

FROM: HEAD OFFICE

DATE: 5 OCTOBER 1999

REF: PRESENTATION

Gemma Ambrose, our Publicity Officer, has been gathering information for a presentation to all regional agents.

We hope that you are able to attend the presentation on Friday 26 November at company headquarters.

MEMORANDUM

TO: ALL STAFF

FROM: GEMMA AMBROSE

DATE: 15 OCTOBER 1999

REF: PRESENTATION TO REGIONAL AGENTS

The presentation date has been set for Friday 26 November.

I will require various reports and documents for this presentation and will be asking you to provide them in due course.

MEMORANDUM

TO: DATA PROCESSING SECTION

FROM: DATA PROCESSING MANAGER

DATE: 18 OCTOBER 1999

REF: UPDATING FILES

Please ensure that you follow existing upper and lower case conventions when updating spreadsheet and database files.

MEMORANDUM

TO: DATA PROCESSING MANAGER

FROM: PROPERTY MAINTENANCE OFFICE

DATE: 19 OCTOBER 1999

REF: REFURBISHED PROPERTY

The following property was inadvertently deleted from all files following flood damage in September. We are pleased to say that it has been completely refurbished. Please add the following details to the relevant database and spreadsheet files.

PROPERTY NAME	HEADLANDS
CODE	S122
LOCATION	SEA
OCCUPANTS	4
BEDROOMS	2
PETS	YES
TV	NO
BOOKED (A)	7
BOOKED (B)	10
PRICE CODE	B
CHANGE DAY	SAT
DATE BOOKED	18 SEP 1999
AGENT	PAUL

Also, please note that you should replicate all necessary formulae when adding new items to the spreadsheet.

When new details are added to the spreadsheet, they must be placed in the correct Location with the existing order of Property Code maintained.

MEMORANDUM

TO: DATA PROCESSING SECTION

FROM: ACCOUNTS SECTION

DATE: 21 OCTOBER 1999

REF: SPREADSHEET AMENDMENTS

Omissions have been identified in the property details spreadsheet. Please check all sections and insert the relevant formulae and functions.

Use the following formulae/functions where appropriate:

SUM
COUNT
LOOKUP

Bookings Section:

Calculate the total number of BOOKED(A) and BOOKED(B) for each of the 6 locations. Display the figures as whole numbers without decimal places.

Properties per Location Section:

Calculate the number of properties per location.

Price Code Details Section:

Name the range of cells containing the price code and cost per week.

Property Details Section:

Calculate the total weeks booked and replicate the formula for each property.

Please calculate the income and replicate the formula for each property. Use the total weeks booked, the price code and the fixed charge. Please note that the fixed charge should only be applied once per property and **NOT** per week booked. The formula must contain the use of the named range together with a lookup function and an absolute cell reference for the fixed charge. Format this data to 2 decimal places without a £ sign.

Calculate the total of the income column and format to currency, showing the £ sign and 2 decimal places.

MEMORANDUM

TO: DATA PROCESSING SECTION

FROM: SALES OFFICE

DATE: 26 OCTOBER 1999

REF: PROPERTY AMENDMENTS

All properties which have BOOKED(A) as 6 should be amended to 7.

MEMORANDUM

TO: DATA PROCESSING SECTION

FROM: SALES OFFICE

DATE: 27 OCTOBER 1999

REF: PROPERTY CHANGE

Details were entered incorrectly for the property below. Please amend the relevant database and spreadsheet files.

	ENTERED AS	SHOULD READ
CODE	M342	M341
BOOKED (A)	8	7
BOOKED (B)	14	13

MEMORANDUM

TO: DATA PROCESSING SECTION

FROM: ACCOUNTS SECTION

DATE: 28 OCTOBER 1999

REF: SPREADSHEET AMENDMENTS

In the TOTAL WEEKS NOT BOOKED column, calculate the total for the first property and replicate the formula for each property. (The maximum number of bookable weeks is 28.)

Add a column after the TOTAL WEEKS NOT BOOKED column, with the heading LOW(A). You must use this column to indicate whether the bookings are less in the BOOKED(A) column than in the BOOKED(B) column.

You will need to use an IF function to give the correct message for each property in this column.

If BOOKED(A) is less than BOOKED(B), then LOW(A) will read 'Yes' otherwise it will read 'No'. Centre the new column heading and messages.

DATA REQUEST FORM

ORIGINATOR Gemma Ambrose   **DATE** 1 Nov 1999

DEPARTMENT Publicity

DATA SOURCE   Spreadsheet ☐   Database ✓

DATA SOURCE   Properties

SEARCH INFORMATION (please complete the relevant boxes)

QUERY

Fields/Headings to Print	All
Sort Order	Ascending order of PROPERTY NAME
Search Criteria	BOOKED(A) 7 or less; PRICE CODE B; DATE BOOKED 18 September 1999 or later
Other Details (please specify)	Field headings must be shown

Printout Required   Yes ✓   No ☐   Fit One Page ✓

REPORT/EXTRACT

Report Format   Group ☐   Column ✓   Tabular ☐

Title	BOOKINGS PERIOD A
Spreadsheet Section	
Fields/Headings to Print	PROPERTY NAME and BOOKED(A) only in this order
Sort Order	PROPERTY NAME descending
Other Details (please specify)	Using the above query, produce a report to be used where specified in the publication

Printout Required   Yes ✓   No ☐   To be dated   Yes ☐   No ✓

Fit One Page   Yes ✓   No ☐   Page Numbered   Yes ☐   No ✓

GRAPH

Title

Axes Labels   Yes ☐   No ☐   Legend Required   Yes ☐   No ☐

Printout Required   Yes ☐   No ☐   Type: Bar/Column ☐   Line ☐   Pie ☐

Other Details (please specify)

DATA REQUEST FORM

ORIGINATOR	Gemma Ambrose	**DATE**	2 Nov 1999
DEPARTMENT	Publicity		
DATA SOURCE	Spreadsheet ☐	Database ✓	
DATA SOURCE	Properties		

SEARCH INFORMATION (please complete the relevant boxes)

QUERY

Fields/Headings to Print	PROPERTY NAME, LOCATION, BOOKED(A), PRICE CODE
Sort Order	Ascending order of PROPERTY NAME
Search Criteria	PROPERTY NAME beginning with the letter S, the letter G or the letter M; LOCATION Sea or Forest; OCCUPANTS 4 or more; CHANGE DAY Saturday; BOOKED(B) more than 8 weeks
Other Details (please specify)	Show only required fields in specified order, including field headings

Printout Required Yes ✓ No ☐   Fit One Page ✓

REPORT/EXTRACT

Report Format   Group ✓   Column ☐   Tabular ☐

Title	BOOKINGS PER LOCATION
Spreadsheet Section	
Fields/Headings to Print	LOCATION, PROPERTY NAME, BOOKED(A)
Sort Order	PROPERTY NAME descending
Other Details (please specify)	Use the above query - group by Location and show totals in BOOKED(A) per region

Printout Required Yes ✓ No ☐   To be dated Yes ✓ No ☐

Fit One Page Yes ✓ No ☐   Page Numbered Yes ✓ No ☐

GRAPH

Title

Axes Labels Yes ☐ No ☐   Legend Required Yes ☐ No ☐

Printout Required Yes ☐ No ☐   Type: Bar/Column ☐   Line ☐   Pie ☐

Other Details (please specify)

DATA REQUEST FORM

ORIGINATOR	Gemma Ambrose	**DATE**	2 Nov 1999
DEPARTMENT	Publicity		

DATA SOURCE Spreadsheet ✓ Database ☐

DATA SOURCE Properties Rental Income

SEARCH INFORMATION (please complete the relevant boxes)

QUERY

Fields/Headings to Print

Sort Order

Search Criteria

Other Details
(please specify)

Printout Required   Yes ☐   No ☐   Fit One Page ☐

REPORT/EXTRACT

Report Format   Group ☐   Column ☐   Tabular ☐

Title

Spreadsheet Section   PROPERTIES PER LOCATION

Fields/Headings to Print   LOCATION, NO OF PROPERTIES

Sort Order

Other Details
(please specify)

Produce and save separately an extract showing the column headings and the detail in these columns for all 6 locations. To be used later where specified in the publication. Do not include the section title in the extract.

Printout Required   Yes ✓   No ☐   To be dated   Yes ☐   No ✓

Fit One Page   Yes ✓   No ☐   Page Numbered   Yes ☐   No ✓

GRAPH

Title   BOOKED(A) AND BOOKED(B) COMPARED

Axes Labels   Yes ✓   No ☐   Legend Required   Yes ✓   No ☐

Printout Required   Yes ✓   No ☐   Type: Bar/Column ☐   Line ✓   Pie ☐

Other Details
(please specify)

Based on Bookings. Compare BOOKED(A) and BOOKED(B) for each location

DATA REQUEST FORM

ORIGINATOR	Gemma Ambrose	**DATE**	3 Nov 1999
DEPARTMENT	Publicity		

DATA SOURCE   Spreadsheet [✓]   Database [ ]

DATA SOURCE   Properties Rental Income

SEARCH INFORMATION (please complete the relevant boxes)

QUERY

Fields/Headings to Print

Sort Order

Search Criteria

Other Details
(please specify)

Printout Required   Yes [ ]   No [ ]   Fit One Page [ ]

REPORT/EXTRACT

Report Format   Group [ ]   Column [ ]   Tabular [ ]

Title

Spreadsheet Section

Fields/Headings to Print

Sort Order

Other Details
(please specify)

Printout Required   Yes [ ]   No [ ]   To be dated   Yes [ ]   No [ ]

Fit One Page   Yes [ ]   No [ ]   Page Numbered   Yes [ ]   No [ ]

GRAPH

Title   BOOKED(A) AND BOOKED(B) COMPARED

Axes Labels   Yes [✓]   No [ ]   Legend Required   Yes [✓]   No [ ]

Printout Required   Yes [✓]   No [ ]   Type: Bar/Column [✓]   Line [ ]   Pie [ ]

Other Details
(please specify)

The wrong type of graph was requested on 2/11/99, please change it. Retain the Y axis minimum value of 0 and increase the maximum to 160. Set intermediate values to intervals of 40. To be used where specified in the presentation.

DATA REQUEST FORM

ORIGINATOR	Gemma Ambrose	**DATE**	5 Nov 1999
DEPARTMENT	Publicity		

DATA SOURCE Spreadsheet ✓   Database ☐

DATA SOURCE Properties Rental Income

SEARCH INFORMATION (please complete the relevant boxes)

QUERY

Fields/Headings to Print

Sort Order

Search Criteria

Other Details
(please specify)

Printout Required   Yes ☐   No ☐   Fit One Page ☐

REPORT/EXTRACT

Report Format   Group ☐   Column ☐   Tabular ☐

Title

Spreadsheet Section   PROPERTY DETAILS

Fields/Headings to Print   LOCATION AND PROPERTY CODE and PRICE CODE

Sort Order

Other Details
(please specify)   Produce an extract showing the details for all properties, in these columns, that have LOW(A) bookings. Do not include the section title in the extract

Printout Required   Yes ✓   No ☐   To be dated   Yes ✓   No ☐

Fit One Page   Yes ✓   No ☐   Page Numbered   Yes ✓   No ☐

GRAPH

Title

Axes Labels   Yes ☐   No ☐   Legend Required   Yes ☐   No ☐

Printout Required   Yes ☐   No ☐   Type: Bar/Column ☐   Line ☐   Pie ☐

Other Details
(please specify)

SOURCE DOCUMENTATION

PRESENTATION

DESIGN BRIEF

DESIGN BRIEF
PRESENTATION

The annual presentation to Regional Offices will take place during November. An automated presentation is to be produced and placed on display at this presentation and at various exhibitions after this date.

You have received, via e-mail, a promotional text file, an extract from which is to be used in the presentation.

You have also received the logo to be used in all promotional materials. This is supplied in corporate colours, but may also be used as a black-and-white or grey image.

Instructions have been given earlier to create a graph from the spreadsheet file, recording the details on your File Store Record Sheet. This graph is to be used in the presentation.

'NATURETRAIL' PROMOTIONAL PRESENTATION

Create a Master slide. Refer to the Presentation House Style Sheets for slide content and instructions on text styles, slide layout and effects. You must ensure that the content of the presentation adheres to Naturetrail's style conventions.

The text content of each slide is given in the Design Brief – Content of the Presentation Slides. Refer to the supplied promotional text file to obtain the extract to be used. The extract text is in the fourth paragraph. Use only the sentence beginning 'We will be continuing.....' and ending '...super cash prizes.'

Refer to your File Store Record Sheet to identify the previously saved graph, and refer to the Content of the Presentation Slides for the position of this graph.

You have discretion (artistic licence) on the final layout of the presentation but this must conform to Naturetrail's House Style Sheets. Select an appropriate point size from the range given in the House Style Sheets, to suit your design.

All presentation material must be checked for spelling before the final draft is approved. Naturetrail's convention is to use open punctuation (eg rather than e.g. and ie rather than i.e.).

DESIGN BRIEF

CONTENT OF THE PRESENTATION SLIDES

Create a Master slide. Please refer to the House Style Sheets to ensure that this adheres to Naturetrail Holidays conventions and for information on slide layout and effects. The text for the automated presentation is given below. You must retain case as shown.

You must create a Master Slide to be used as a background for all 5 slides.

SLIDE NO	TYPE OF ENTRY	SLIDE CONTENT	SLIDE DURATION
Master Slide	Master Slide Text	*Specified text and image – see House Style Sheet 2* Slide Layout and Effects for details	

SLIDE NO	TYPE OF ENTRY	SLIDE CONTENT	SLIDE DURATION
Slide 1	Heading Heading	NATURETRAIL HOLIDAYS TOTAL RELAXATION	7 – 15 secs
Slide 2	Heading Heading Subheading Subheading	A PERFECT HOLIDAY PHONE NOW Tel: 01234 29786 Open 7 am to 7 pm	7 – 15 secs
Slide 3	Heading Body text (Bullet text)	BEAUTIFUL LOCATIONS Our holiday homes are situated in some of the most delightful settings, for example: Rivers Lakes Sea Mountains	15 – 20 secs
Slide 4	Heading Body text Graph	RESERVATIONS Why not take a holiday in the spring when there is usually more choice: *Insert graph here*	10 – 20 secs
Slide 5	Heading Heading Subheading Extract text	PREVIOUS CUSTOMER? EXTRA SAVINGS! Contact us now! *Extract text from text file as specified in Design Brief*	15 – 25 secs

HOUSE STYLE SHEET 1   PRESENTATION TEXT STYLES

STYLE NAME	TYPEFACE	POINT SIZE	FEATURE	ALIGNMENT	ADDITIONAL
Master Slide text	Any	Between 12 – 16 pt	Any	-	All Master slide text must be the same style and consistent throughout the presentation
Heading	Sans serif	Between 40 – 60 pt	Bold	Centre	Consistent throughout the presentation
Subheading	Sans serif	Between 26 – 36 pt	Italic	Centre	Consistent throughout the presentation
Body text	Serif	Between 18 – 24 pt	None	Left	Consistent throughout the presentation
Bullet text	Serif	Between 18 – 24 pt	Italic	Left	No more than 6 bullet points per slide
Extract text	Sans serif	Between 18 – 24 pt	Bold	Left	Consistent throughout the presentation. **DO NOT** apply to any text included in imported image or graph

COPYFITTING

- Text and imported data are adjusted so that they are not superimposed on other text or data

- Imported data must not be split across slides

HOUSE STYLE SHEET 2

PRESENTATION SLIDE LAYOUT AND EFFECTS

FEATURE	COLOUR	STYLE	POSITION	MAX NUMBER	ADDITIONAL
Background	Any	Any	-	1	Consistent use throughout the presentation
Data on Master Slide	Any – see ADDITIONAL column	-	-	2 text colours	Consistent use throughout the presentation Ensure legibility against background colour/style To contain the organisation's logo, the name of the organisation, name of designer and the date
Text	Any – see ADDITIONAL column	-	-	2 colours	Consistent use throughout the presentation Ensure legibility against background colour/style
Logo	Corporate colours or black and white	-	Master Slide	-	Consistent use throughout the presentation and original proportions maintained
Images, diagrams or graphs	Any	-	As specified in Design Brief	As specified in Design Brief	Original proportions must be maintained at all times
Transitions	-	-	-	4 effects	At least 2 different effects must be used
Builds	-	-	-	4 effects	At least 2 different effects must be used

SOURCE DOCUMENTATION

PUBLICATION

DESIGN BRIEF

DESIGN BRIEF

PUBLICATION

This year's annual presentation will address the issues of promotional literature. An A4 4-page publication is to be produced to send out to potential customers as a follow up to our annual brochure.

Included in your files you received via e-mail was a text file, which is to be used in the publication. A hard copy of this file is supplied in this Design Brief for reference.

You have also received the logo to be used in all promotional materials. This is supplied in corporate colours, but may also be used as a black and white or grey image.

You have been given instructions earlier to extract and save data from the database and spreadsheet files, recording these details on your File Store Record Sheet. These extracts are to be used in the publication.

'NATURETRAIL' PROMOTIONAL PUBLICATION

Create a front cover. This will be the first page of the 4-page publication. Ensure that it contains only the logo, as instructed in the Publication House Style Sheet 1.

On the second page use the headline **Naturetrail News**. Import the text file directly below the headline.

You have discretion (artistic licence) on the final layout of the publication but this must conform to Naturetrail's House Style Sheets.

Refer to the hard copy of the text file enclosed with this Brief, this shows the placement of the extracts from the database and spreadsheet files, the logo and the bulleted text.

GENERAL

All publication material must be checked for spelling before final draft is approved. Naturetrail's convention is to use open punctuation (eg rather than e.g. and ie rather than i.e.).

COPYFITTING

- Headings/subheadings must not be split from the related text
- Line spacing between subheadings, paragraphs and imported data must be applied consistently
- One line or less of text is grouped with the rest of related text ('widows and orphans')
- No more than two clear lines of white space are left at the end of columns throughout the document, the only exception is at the end of the publication.
- Text and imported data are adjusted so that they are not superimposed on other text or data
- Imported data must not be split across columns or pages

TEXT FOR PUBLICATION

If you are looking for a peaceful and relaxing holiday then look no further than Naturetrail Holidays. From small beginnings five years ago when the company had only one location we are now able to offer a choice of six completely different locations. Whatever your idea of the perfect place for a holiday we have the answer.

LOCATIONS

We have holiday cottages in the beautiful unspoit countryside of the Cotswolds. Here you are able to ramble along the picturesque footpaths and visit the charming villages and small towns that are dotted around this area. Our forest properties are situated in North Wales, close to Betws-y-Coed. There are endless outdoor activites in this area ranging from walking, canoeing or climing. In Cumbria you will find our lakes cottages – if you like sailing and fishing then this is the place for you. Again in North Wales, situated in the heart of Snowdonia, you will find our mountain complex. There are even trained mountaineers on hand to give you coaching in all aspects of climbing. So don't worry if you're a novice, there are activities ranging from those for beginers right through to the more experienced climber. Cornwall is the setting for our seaside properties. These are located between Boscastle and Newquay. The scenery in this area is second to none. There are wild coastal footpaths, fishing villages and sandy beaches. You will be spoilt for choice for your daily excursions! For those of you who enjoy the tranquillity of a riverside setting, you will find this at our site in Devon. Our properties are situated only 100 metres from the river Dart. Of course also in this area, in addition to riverside activities, there are beautiful moorland walks.

THE CHOICE IS YOURS. We beleve that you cannot fail to appreciate the natural beauty that abounds in all of these locations.

Insert logo here →

PROPERTIES AVAILABLE

Our properties vary in size and we have properties to suit most needs. You can choose from one to four bedrooms, with the maximum occupancy being eight people (there is the possibility that some of our properties can accommodate babies – cots and high chairs can be provided at no extra cost). Please ask the agent when booking.

PRICES

Prices vary depending on the size of the property. This year we have introduced a new system and now if you book for more than one week, any subsequent weeks are charged at a reduced rate.

The table below shows the prices relating to the different codes:

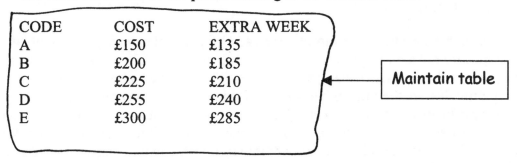

CODE	COST	EXTRA WEEK
A	£150	£135
B	£200	£185
C	£225	£210
D	£255	£240
E	£300	£285

Maintain table

Insert database report here

Why not reserve a property for our early booking period? The properties shown below are on special discount prices (deduct a further 10% from the price shown in the brochure) for this year only:

You can arrive on Friday or Saturday depending on which property you have chosen and at any time before 7 pm. Please let us know if you will be arriving later than this. Staggering arrivals in this way makes it easier to ensure that we have more staff available to give you a warm welcome. You may prefer to travel on a Friday, especially in summer when the roads are usually less congested. Whilst on the subject of transport, you will notice that most of our properties have parking adjacent to them. Where this is not the case your vehicle may be left in the parking areas which are never more than 50 metres away. For unloading purposes, parking outside the property is perfectly acceptable but please remember to move your vehicle as soon as you can since it will cause an obstruction.

Your property will have been fully cleaned and inspected beffore your arrival which can be anytime after 12 noon. All bed linen is provided but you will need to bring your own towels. All properties are self-catering but to help you settle in, we do provide a small grocery basket containing essentials, such as bread and milk. Should you find that things are not to your liking, please contact us straight away. WE PRIDE OURSELVES ON GIVING YOU THE BEST SERVICE AT ALL TIMES.

LOYALTY SAVINGS

Naturetrail Holidays are pleased to to announce an important bonus for customers who have taken holidays with us in the past. We are now able to give substantial discounts on your holiday booking this year.

If you book your holiday before the end of January you will be entitled to a 20% discount on the standard cost of your chosen property (subject to its availability). If you book before the end of March you will be entitled to a 10% discount on the standard cost.

We feel that this is a very generous ofer and hope that you will be able to make your bookings early to benefit from the maximum savings.

Each 'loyalty' customer will be entered into our prize draw. We will be offering cash prizes ranging from £50 to £500 to those lucky ones picked out at random. If you are eligible for this discount please have your previous booking reference to hand when you call. If you no longer have your booking reference, don't worry we will be able to look up your details on our database.

HOW TO BOOK

Our properties can be booked from our Head Office by telephoning 01234 29786. We are open from 7 am to 7 pm every day except Sunday. Our regional offices can also help you with any queries that you may have. They are each allocated several properties that are their major concern. Choosing the right accomodation to suit your needs can be difficult and we want to help you make an informed choice. You can rely on our staff giving informative and friendly advice. Our computerised booking system gives instant availability of our properties so that we can suggest an alternative should your first choice be taken. Shown below are the properties dealt with by our Bristol office:

Insert spreadsheet report here

As you can see each regional office deals with properties from all of the locations. Our staff training ensures that all staff have visited the six locations and are aware of the differences between them.

When booking please ensure that you have the following details to hand:

Bullet text

Reference of Property
Price Code
Date Required
Number in Party
Vehicle Registration Number
Credit Card Number
Former Booking Ref (if applicable)

Here at Naturetrail Holidays we pride ourselves in providing an excelent booking service and we hope that you feel that this level of excellence carries through to all of our operations. We know how important it is that everything runs smoothly so that you are able to relax and enjoy yourselves.

So what are you waiting for? Have another look through our brochure and imagiine the fun that you'll have with Naturetrail Holidays.

DON'T DELAY – BOOK TODAY.

HOUSE STYLE SHEET 1   PUBLICATION PAGE LAYOUT

FEATURE	MEASUREMENT	POSITION	ADDITIONAL
Margins	1.5 cm left and right 1.5 cm top and bottom	-	Consistent throughout the publication
Spacing between Columns	1.5 cm	-	Consistent between all columns
Page Numbering	10 pt	At top of page	Not to be printed on front cover. To commence with number 2 on second page Align consistently throughout the publication
Headers/Footers	10 pt	-	Footer should contain the name of the designer and the date of the publication
Pages	A4	-	Consistent orientation throughout the publication – either portrait or landscape
Columns	-	-	2 – 4 columns for all text except the headline Columns should be of equal size throughout the publication
Logo/Image	On front cover – this should cover at least half of the width of the page When used elsewhere in the document it must be centred within the column	On front cover, centre horizontally, either within margins or page. It need not be centred vertically Elsewhere, position as specified in Text For Publication	Logo must always appear in full. Original proportions must be maintained at all times When in colour only corporate colours may be used Black and white image may be used if preferred

HOUSE STYLE SHEET 2   PUBLICATION TEXT STYLE

STYLE NAME	TYPEFACE	POINT SIZE	FEATURE	ALIGNMENT	ADDITIONAL
Headline	Sans serif	Between 36-60 pt	Bold Capitals	Centre	Position horizontally across the page or margins. Must be across full width of page spanning all columns
Subheading	Sans serif	Between 16-22 pt	Italic	Centre	Consistent throughout the publication DO NOT apply to text included within imported graphs, images or diagrams
Body text	Serif	Between 10-14 pt	-	Left	Consistent throughout the publication. Set in 2 – 4 columns
Bullet text	Serif	Use same as body text (between 10-14 pt)	To include a bullet character (eg ● ◆ □)	Left	Ensure the bullet text is indented from the bullet point (hanging indent) Consistent throughout
Extract text	Sans serif	Between 10-14 pt	Bold	Any	Extract style applies to all extracted text, except text included within graphs, images or diagrams DO NOT exceed column width Consistent throughout the publication Place a box or border around the text

Syllabus for IBT III

1 Electronic communications

ASSESSMENT OBJECTIVES	SYLLABUS CONTENT
The Candidate must be able to:	❑ total coverage • selective coverage – selective coverage
1.1 Communicate electronically	
1.1a Create and transmit e-mail message(s) attaching files as required	❑ use e-mail • access received message(s) and files • create message(s)
1.1b Correctly route/address e-mail message(s)	• route/address message(s) • attach files to message(s)
1.1c Retrieve e-mail message(s) and access the attached files	• transmit message(s) • print message(s) including records of transaction(s)
1.1d Print e-mail message(s) including records of transaction(s) and evidence of attachments	• forward message • reply to sender

2 File management

ASSESSMENT OBJECTIVES	SYLLABUS CONTENT

The Candidate must be able to:

❑ total coverage • selective coverage
– selective coverage

2.1 Create, manage and maintain files

2.1a Create and name directories/folders/files as required

2.1b Manage files and documents within directories/folders as specified

2.1c Record storage details

❑ create directories/folders
❑ create subdirectories/folders
❑ manage files/documents
• save/name
– files – queries – reports – sheets – charts
• retrieve
– files – queries – reports – sheets – charts
• copy/move
– files – queries – reports – sheets – charts
• delete
– files
❑ record storage details
– files – queries – reports – sheets – charts

3 Source data processing

ASSESSMENT OBJECTIVES	SYLLABUS CONTENT
The Candidate must be able to: **3.1 Analyse task(s), select and process the relevant data**	❑ total coverage • selective coverage – selective coverage
3.1a Select, locate and access correct data 3.1b Process data as specified, to the required accuracy	❑ access existing files • text • database • spreadsheet • image ❑ process existing files • insert data – records – columns – rows • edit data – text – numeric • delete data – records – columns – fields – rows • find and replace facility • format data areas – decimal places – integer – currency – case – alignment – borders – shading – font – character – size

ASSESSMENT OBJECTIVES	SYLLABUS CONTENT
The Candidate must be able to:	❑ total coverage • selective coverage – selective coverage
3.2 Interrogate, manipulate and present data	
3.2a Create and run queries containing up to five specified criteria	❑ create and run queries • search using: – logical operators – text – numeric or data range – wildcard
3.2b Correct use of formulae and functions to provide the required solutions	• sort – ascending – descending – alphabetically/numerically
3.2c Create graph(s) with the required accuracy, to display data as specified	❑ use formulae and functions • absolute cell addresses • relative cell addresses
3.2d Transfer data between files	• named cells/ranges • functions
3.2e Create reports with the required accuracy, to display data as specified	– sum – average – count – lookup – if • replicate formulae ❑ create graphs

3.2f Print required data as specified	• select type
	  – line – area – bar – pie – comparative
	• apply labels and legends
	• control y-axis range
	• control y-axis intervals
	❑ transfer data between files/applications
	• transfer data
	  – copy – cut – paste – paste special (values)
	❑ create and generate reports
	• design/select layout
	• display selected fields/cells
	• group by categories
	• total, count or average specified data
	• format data – decimal places – interger – currency – case – alignment
	• enter data
	• hide data
	❑ print data
	• sheets
	• extracts
	• formulae
	• reports
	• queries
	• graphs

4 Automated presentation production

ASSESSMENT OBJECTIVES	SYLLABUS CONTENT
The Candidate must be able to: **4.1 Set up master slide in accordance with a specified house style**	❏ total coverage ● selective coverage – selective coverage

4.1a Set up master slide in accordance with a specified house style	❏ layout
	● text
	   – headings – sub-headings – body text – bulleted text
	● indents/tabs
	● graphics
	   – images
	❏ styles
	● background
	● text
	   – headings – sub-headings – body text – bulleted text – extracts
	● colours
	● point size
	● serif and sans serif fonts
	● text alignment
	● text enhancement
	   – bold – italic – underline

ASSESSMENT OBJECTIVES	SYLLABUS CONTENT

4.2 Insert, manipulate and produce a presentation

4.2a Produce a presentation in accordance with a given design brief in a specified house style
 	
4.2b Present required data as specified
	❑ enter text
	❑ transfer data between files/applications
	● transfer data
	   – copy/cut/paste – import – export
	❑ manipulate and present data
	● copyfit material
	   – consistent spacing within a style area –
	   text/images/lines not superimposed – imported
	   images and/or extracts not split across slides
	● control sizes of image(s) in proportion
	● spellcheck
	● slide order – set up – change
	❑ effects
	● transitional effects (up to four)
	● transitional timings (various specified)
	● build effects (up to four)
	❑ provide specified output
	● automated presentation – run – loop
	● print
	   – slides – thumbnails – notes

5 Publication production

ASSESSMENT OBJECTIVES	SYLLABUS CONTENT
The Candidate must be able to:	❏ total coverage ● selective coverage – selective coverage
5.1 Set up document layout and styles	

5.1a Set up document(s) in accordance with a specified house style	❏ layout
	● margins
	  – left – right – top – bottom
	● columns
	  – two to four columns – column spacing
	● page
	  – orientation – size
	● multiple pages
	● page numbering
	  – position – first page excluded – start number (other than one)
	● headers/footers
	● indents/tabs
	❏ styles
	● categories
	  – headline – sub-headings – body – bullets – extracts – headers/footers
	● borders/lines
	● point sizes
	● serif and sans serif fonts
	● line spacing
	● text alignment
	● text enhancement
	  – italic – bold

ASSESSMENT OBJECTIVES	SYLLABUS CONTENT

5.2   Insert, manipulate and present data

5.2a   Produce document(s) in accordance with a given design brief in a specified house style

5.2b   Print required data as specified

- ❑ enter text
- ● enter
- ● delete
- ● cut – copy/cut/paste
- ❑ transfer data between files/applications
- ● transfer data
  - – copy – cut and paste – import – export
- ❑ manipulate and present data
- ● copyfit material
  - – widows/orphans – consistent spacing – group headings/sub-headings with related data – text/images/lines not superimposed – imported images and/or extracts not split across columns/pages – control white space (ie no more than two blank lines at the bottom of any but the final column)
- ● control size(s) of image(s) in proportion
- ● spellcheck
- ● use drawing features
  - – lines – circles – boxes – ellipses – shading/fill/pattern
- ❑ print

IBT III assessment procedures

The assessment consists of one practical assignment, similar to that given in Part 2. This takes place at the end of a course of study. Once candidates start the assignment, no further tuition can be given. No help, other than that for technical failure of equipment, can be given during the assessment. Candidates are allowed limited feedback on the source data processing action. This must be shown to your tutor before progressing.

The candidate is allowed a total of ten hours to complete all the components, spread over sessions to suit the centre and candidates. Ten hours is usually ample time for most candidates. The Time Log Sheet must be completed at the end of each session so that there is a running total. Printing can be done outside the ten hours.

The assessment must be supervised, as with CLAIT and IBT II assessments, but strict examination conditions are not necessary.

Your tutor will be able to advise you of the exact procedures for your situation.

Answers to exercises

Chapter 3, Section 2, Exercise 1

PROPERTY NAME	CODE	LOCATION	OCCUPANTS	BEDROOMS	BOOKED(A)	BOOKED(B)	PRICE CODE	TV	CHANGE DAY	DATE BOOKED	AGENT
PEANUTS	F919	FOREST	4	2	7	12	B	☐	SAT	18-Sep-99	PAUL
ASPENS	M340	MOUNTAIN	2	1	7	10	B	☐	FRI	24-Sep-99	JANE
HEADLANDS	R691	RIVERS	4	2	7	12	B	☐	SAT	18-Sep-99	PAUL
PUFFINS	S855	SEA	4	1	5	14	B	☐	SAT	25-Sep-99	MIKE

Chapter 3, Section 2, Exercise 2

PROPERTY NAME	LOCATION	BOOKED(A)	PRICE CODE
SURF	SEA	11	C
STARFISH	SEA	7	C
SHRIMPS	SEA	7	C
SHINGLE	SEA	11	C
SHELLFISH	SEA	11	C
SEASHORE	SEA	12	E
MUSSELS	SEA	10	C
MOLLUSCS	SEA	13	D
MISTY	SEA	12	D
MARBLE	FOREST	11	C

Chapter 3, Section 2, Exercise 3

PROPERTY NAME	LOCATION	BOOKED(A)	CHANGE DAY	AGENT
PEANUTS	FOREST	7	SAT	PAUL
SPARROWS	LAKES	7	SAT	PAUL
STARFISH	SEA	7	SAT	PAUL
OYSTERS	SEA	7	FRI	GAIL
BANANAS	MOUNTAIN	7	FRI	PAUL
HEADLANDS	RIVERS	7	SAT	PAUL
WATERFALLS	FOREST	7	SAT	PAUL
PARSLEY	LAKES	7	FRI	PAUL
WALNUTS	LAKES	7	FRI	PAUL
BEECHES	LAKES	8	FRI	PAUL
BEIGE	COUNTRY	8	SAT	GAIL
PRUNES	COUNTRY	9	FRI	PAUL
ULTRAMARINE	SEA	9	FRI	GAIL
BRONZE	MOUNTAIN	9	SAT	PAUL
LIMES	RIVERS	10	FRI	PAUL
PAWPAWS	SEA	10	FRI	PAUL
ISLANDS	SEA	11	SAT	PAUL
RAISINS	COUNTRY	11	FRI	PAUL
LIMPETS	SEA	12	FRI	GAIL
REDWINGS	RIVERS	12	FRI	PAUL
RIVERS	RIVERS	12	FRI	PAUL
MINT	COUNTRY	12	FRI	PAUL
SEA URCHINS	SEA	14	FRI	PAUL
BLACKCURRANTS	COUNTRY	14	SAT	PAUL
CINNABAR	LAKES	14	FRI	PAUL
CLIFFS	SEA	14	FRI	PAUL
THYME	COUNTRY	14	FRI	PAUL
PLUMS	COUNTRY	14	FRI	PAUL
BISCUIT	MOUNTAIN	14	FRI	PAUL

Chapter 3, Section 2

QUERY DESIGNS

NOTE: Only fields with sorting and a criteria search are shown.

Chapter 3 Section 2.2 QUERY 1

Field:	CODE	BOOKED(A)	PRICE CODE	DATE BOOKED
Table:	Holiday homes	Holiday homes	Holiday homes	Holiday homes
Sort:	Ascending			
Show:	☑	☑	☑	☑
Criteria:		<=7	"B"	>#17/09/99#

Chapter 3 Section 2.2 QUERY 2

PROPERTY NAME	LOCATION	OCCUPANTS	CHANGE DAY	BOOKED (B)
Holiday homes	Holiday homes	Holiday homes	Holiday homes	Holiday home
Descending				
☑	☑	☐	☐	☐
Like "S*" Or Like "G*" Or Like "M*"	"SEA" Or "FOREST"	> =4	"SAT"	>8

Chapter 3 Section 2.2 QUERY 3

Field:	BOOKED(A)	AGENT	BOOKED(B)
Table:	Holiday homes	Holiday homes	Holiday homes
Sort:	Ascending		
Show:	☑	☑	☐
Criteria:	>6 And <15	"PAUL" Or "GAIL"	>=12

Chapter 3, Section 2, Exercise 4

LOW BOOKINGS PERIOD A

PROPERTY NAME   ASPENS

BOOKED (A)   7

PROPERTY NAME   HEADLANDS

BOOKED (A)   7

PROPERTY NAME   PEANUTS

BOOKED (A)   7

PROPERTY NAME   PUFFINS

BOOKED (A)   5

Chapter 3, Section 2, Exercise 5

BOOKINGS PER LOCATION

LOCATION	PROPERTY NAME	BOOKED (A)
COUNTRY		
	BEIGE	8
	BLACKCURRANTS	14
	MINT	12
	PLUMS	14
	PRUNES	9
	RAISINS	11
	THYME	14
		82
FOREST		
	PEANUTS	7
	WATERFALLS	7
		14
LAKES		
	BEECHES	8
	CINNABAR	14
	PARSLEY	7
	SPARROWS	7
	WALNUTS	7
		43
MOUNTAIN		
	BANANAS	7
	BISCUIT	14
	BRONZE	9
		30
RIVERS		
	HEADLANDS	7
	LIMES	10
	REDWINGS	12
	RIVERS	12
		41
SEA		
	CLIFFS	14
	ISLANDS	11
	LIMPETS	12
	OYSTERS	7
	PAWPAWS	10
	SEA URCHINS	14
	STARFISH	7
	ULTRAMARINE	9
		84

Chapter 3, Section 2, Exercise 5

Chapter 4, Section 1, Exercise 5

NATURETRAIL HOLIDAYS										
ANALYSIS OF INCOME										
								BOOKINGS		
PRICE CODE DETAILS									BOOKED(A)	BOOKED(B)
PRICE CODE		A	B	C	D	E				
COST PER WEEK(£)		150.00	200.00	225.00	255.00	300.00	COUNTRY			
							FOREST			
FIXED CHARGE(£)		50.00					LAKES			
							MOUNTAIN			
							RIVERS			
							SEA			
PROPERTY DETAILS										
LOCATION AND PROPERTY CODE	BOOKED(A)	BOOKED(B)	PRICE CODE	TOTAL WEEKS BOOKED	INCOME	TOTAL WEEKS NOT BOOKED				
COUNTRY										
C181	12	12	B							
C34	14	12	B							
C66	14	9	B							
C670	11	14	B							
C777	9	12	B							
C91	14	12	D							
C997	14	14	C							
FOREST										
F129	7	13	A							
F642	7	14	C							
F919	7	12	B							
LAKES										
L654	12	10	C							
L67	7	14	C							
L801	14	14	A							
L802	8	14	B							
L816	7	13	A							
L817	11	11	A							
L855	11	6	B							
L919	7	14	D							
MOUNTAIN										
M30	7	13	A							
M341	7	13	B							
M443	9	11	E							
M45	9	6	A							
M51	14	9	E							
M666	9	11	B							
M88	9	12	E							
M89	11	9	B							
M975	14	14	A							
RIVERS										
R103	14	14	E							
R134	12	14	B							
R21	14	12	C							
R54	12	14	B							
R691	7	12	B							
SEA										
S126	11	12	E							
S16	7	14	C							
S222	14	12	D							
S51	14	14	E							
S555	10	14	C							
S589	14	10	E							
S715	12	12	D							
S89	13	14	D							
				TOTAL(£)						
PROPERTIES PER LOCATION										
LOCATION	NO OF PROPERTIES									
COUNTRY										
FOREST										
LAKES										
MOUNTAIN										
RIVERS										
SEA										

Chapter 4, Section 2, Exercise 11

NATURETRAIL HOLIDAYS									
ANALYSIS OF INCOME									
							BOOKINGS		
		PRICE CODE DETAILS						BOOKED(A)	BOOKED(B)
PRICE CODE		A	B	C	D	E			
COST PER WEEK(£)		150.00	200.00	225.00	255.00	300.00	COUNTRY	88	85
							FOREST	21	39
FIXED CHARGE(£)		50.00					LAKES	77	96
							MOUNTAIN	89	98
							RIVERS	59	66
							SEA	95	102
			PROPERTY DETAILS						
LOCATION AND PROPERTY CODE	BOOKED(A)	BOOKED(B)	PRICE CODE	TOTAL WEEKS BOOKED	INCOME	TOTAL WEEKS NOT BOOKED	LOW(A)		
COUNTRY									
C181	12	12	B	24	4850.00	4	NO		
C34	14	12	B	26	5250.00	2	NO		
C66	14	9	B	23	4650.00	5	NO		
C670	11	14	B	25	5050.00	3	YES		
C777	9	12	B	21	4250.00	7	YES		
C91	14	12	D	26	6680.00	2	NO		
C997	14	14	C	28	6350.00	0	NO		
FOREST									
F129	7	13	A	20	3050.00	8	YES		
F642	7	14	C	21	4775.00	7	YES		
F919	7	12	B	19	3850.00	9	YES		
LAKES									
L654	12	10	C	22	5000.00	6	NO		
L67	7	14	C	21	4775.00	7	YES		
L801	14	14	A	28	4250.00	0	NO		
L802	8	14	B	22	4450.00	6	YES		
L816	7	13	A	20	3050.00	8	YES		
L817	11	11	A	22	3350.00	6	NO		
L855	11	6	B	17	3450.00	11	NO		
L919	7	14	D	21	5405.00	7	YES		
MOUNTAIN									
M30	7	13	A	20	3050.00	8	YES		
M341	7	13	B	20	4050.00	8	YES		
M443	9	11	E	20	6050.00	8	YES		
M45	9	6	A	15	2300.00	13	NO		
M51	14	9	E	23	6950.00	5	NO		
M666	9	11	B	20	4050.00	8	YES		
M88	9	12	E	21	6350.00	7	YES		
M89	11	9	B	20	4050.00	8	NO		
M975	14	14	A	28	4250.00	0	NO		
RIVERS									
R103	14	14	E	28	8450.00	0	NO		
R134	12	14	B	26	5250.00	2	YES		
R21	14	12	C	26	5900.00	2	NO		
R54	12	14	B	26	5250.00	2	YES		
R691	7	12	B	19	3850.00	9	YES		
SEA									
S126	11	12	E	23	6950.00	5	YES		
S16	7	14	C	21	4775.00	7	YES		
S222	14	12	D	26	6680.00	2	NO		
S51	14	14	E	28	8450.00	0	NO		
S555	10	14	C	24	5450.00	4	YES		
S589	14	10	E	24	7250.00	4	NO		
S715	12	12	D	24	6170.00	4	NO		
S89	13	14	D	27	6935.00	1	YES		
				TOTAL(£)	£204,945.00				
PROPERTIES PER LOCATION									
LOCATION	NO OF PROPERTIES								
COUNTRY	7								
FOREST	3								
LAKES	8								
MOUNTAIN	9								
RIVERS	5								
SEA	8								
AVERAGE	7								

Chapter 4, Section 2, Exercise 12

NATURETRA									BOOKED(A)	BOOKED(B)
ANALYSIS O										
								BOOKINGS		
				PRICE CODE DETAILS					BOOKED(A)	BOOKED(B)
PRICE CODE		A	B	C		D	E			
COST PER WEEK		150	200	225	255		300	COUNTRY	=SUM(B18:B24)	=SUM(C18:C24)
								FOREST	=SUM(B26:B28)	=SUM(C26:C28)
FIXED CHARGE(£)		50						LAKES	=SUM(B30:B37)	=SUM(C30:C37)
								MOUNTAIN	=SUM(B39:B47)	=SUM(C39:C47)
								RIVERS	=SUM(B49:B53)	=SUM(C49:C53)
								SEA	=SUM(B55:B62)	=SUM(C55:C62)

				PROPERTY DETAILS					
LOCATION AND PROPERTY CODE	BOOKED(A)	BOOKED	PRICE	TOTAL WEEKS BOOKED	INCOME	TOTAL WEEKS NOT BOOKED	LOW(A)		
COUNTRY									
C181	12	12	B	=SUM(B18:C18)	=E18*LOOKUP(D18,CODE)+$C$10	=28-E18	=IF(B18<C18,"YES","NO")		
C34	14	12	B	=SUM(B19:C19)	=E19*LOOKUP(D19,CODE)+$C$10	=28-E19	=IF(B19<C19,"YES","NO")		
C66	14	9	B	=SUM(B20:C20)	=E20*LOOKUP(D20,CODE)+$C$10	=28-E20	=IF(B20<C20,"YES","NO")		
C670	11	14	B	=SUM(B21:C21)	=E21*LOOKUP(D21,CODE)+$C$10	=28-E21	=IF(B21<C21,"YES","NO")		
C777	9	12	B	=SUM(B22:C22)	=E22*LOOKUP(D22,CODE)+$C$10	=28-E22	=IF(B22<C22,"YES","NO")		
C91	14	12	D	=SUM(B23:C23)	=E23*LOOKUP(D23,CODE)+$C$10	=28-E23	=IF(B23<C23,"YES","NO")		
C997	14	14	C	=SUM(B24:C24)	=E24*LOOKUP(D24,CODE)+$C$10	=28-E24	=IF(B24<C24,"YES","NO")		
FOREST									
F129	7	13	A	=SUM(B26:C26)	=E26*LOOKUP(D26,CODE)+$C$10	=28-E26	=IF(B26<C26,"YES","NO")		
F642	7	14	C	=SUM(B27:C27)	=E27*LOOKUP(D27,CODE)+$C$10	=28-E27	=IF(B27<C27,"YES","NO")		
F919	7	12	B	=SUM(B28:C28)	=E28*LOOKUP(D28,CODE)+$C$10	=28-E28	=IF(B28<C28,"YES","NO")		
LAKES									
L654	12	10	C	=SUM(B30:C30)	=E30*LOOKUP(D30,CODE)+$C$10	=28-E30	=IF(B30<C30,"YES","NO")		
L67	7	14	C	=SUM(B31:C31)	=E31*LOOKUP(D31,CODE)+$C$10	=28-E31	=IF(B31<C30,"YES","NO")		
L801	14	14	A	=SUM(B32:C32)	=E32*LOOKUP(D32,CODE)+$C$10	=28-E32	=IF(B32<C32,"YES","NO")		
L802	8	14	B	=SUM(B33:C33)	=E33*LOOKUP(D33,CODE)+$C$10	=28-E33	=IF(B33<C33,"YES","NO")		
L816	7	13	A	=SUM(B34:C34)	=E34*LOOKUP(D34,CODE)+$C$10	=28-E34	=IF(B34<C34,"YES","NO")		
L817	11	11	A	=SUM(B35:C35)	=E35*LOOKUP(D35,CODE)+$C$10	=28-E35	=IF(B35<C35,"YES","NO")		
L855	11	6	B	=SUM(B36:C36)	=E36*LOOKUP(D36,CODE)+$C$10	=28-E36	=IF(B36<C36,"YES","NO")		
L919	7	14	D	=SUM(B37:C37)	=E37*LOOKUP(D37,CODE)+$C$10	=28-E37	=IF(B37<C37,"YES","NO")		
MOUNTAIN									
M30	7	13	A	=SUM(B39:C39)	=E39*LOOKUP(D39,CODE)+$C$10	=28-E39	=IF(B39<C39,"YES","NO")		
M341	7	13	B	=SUM(B40:C40)	=E40*LOOKUP(D40,CODE)+$C$10	=28-E40	=IF(B40<C40,"YES","NO")		
M443	9	11	E	=SUM(B41:C41)	=E41*LOOKUP(D41,CODE)+$C$10	=28-E41	=IF(B41<C41,"YES","NO")		
M45	9	6	A	=SUM(B42:C42)	=E42*LOOKUP(D42,CODE)+$C$10	=28-E42	=IF(B42<C42,"YES","NO")		
M51	14	9	E	=SUM(B43:C43)	=E43*LOOKUP(D43,CODE)+$C$10	=28-E43	=IF(B43<C43,"YES","NO")		
M666	9	11	B	=SUM(B44:C44)	=E44*LOOKUP(D44,CODE)+$C$10	=28-E44	=IF(B44<C44,"YES","NO")		
M88	9	12	E	=SUM(B45:C45)	=E45*LOOKUP(D45,CODE)+$C$10	=28-E45	=IF(B45<C45,"YES","NO")		
M89	11	9	B	=SUM(B46:C46)	=E46*LOOKUP(D46,CODE)+$C$10	=28-E46	=IF(B46<C46,"YES","NO")		
M975	14	14	A	=SUM(B47:C47)	=E47*LOOKUP(D47,CODE)+$C$10	=28-E47	=IF(B47<C47,"YES","NO")		
RIVERS									
R103	14	14	E	=SUM(B49:C49)	=E49*LOOKUP(D49,CODE)+$C$10	=28-E49	=IF(B49<C49,"YES","NO")		
R134	12	14	B	=SUM(B50:C50)	=E50*LOOKUP(D50,CODE)+$C$10	=28-E50	=IF(B50<C50,"YES","NO")		
R21	14	12	C	=SUM(B51:C51)	=E51*LOOKUP(D51,CODE)+$C$10	=28-E51	=IF(B51<C51,"YES","NO")		
R54	12	14	B	=SUM(B52:C52)	=E52*LOOKUP(D52,CODE)+$C$10	=28-E52	=IF(B52<C52,"YES","NO")		
R691	7	12	B	=SUM(B53:C53)	=E53*LOOKUP(D53,CODE)+$C$10	=28-E53	=IF(B53<C53,"YES","NO")		
SEA									
S126	11	12	E	=SUM(B55:C55)	=E55*LOOKUP(D55,CODE)+$C$10	=28-E55	=IF(B55<C55,"YES","NO")		
S16	7	14	C	=SUM(B56:C56)	=E56*LOOKUP(D56,CODE)+$C$10	=28-E56	=IF(B56<C56,"YES","NO")		
S222	14	12	D	=SUM(B57:C57)	=E57*LOOKUP(D57,CODE)+$C$10	=28-E57	=IF(B57<C57,"YES","NO")		
S51	14	14	E	=SUM(B58:C58)	=E58*LOOKUP(D58,CODE)+$C$10	=28-E58	=IF(B58<C58,"YES","NO")		
S555	10	14	C	=SUM(B59:C59)	=E59*LOOKUP(D59,CODE)+$C$10	=28-E59	=IF(B59<C59,"YES","NO")		
S589	14	10	E	=SUM(B60:C60)	=E60*LOOKUP(D60,CODE)+$C$10	=28-E60	=IF(B60<C60,"YES","NO")		
S715	12	12	D	=SUM(B61:C61)	=E61*LOOKUP(D61,CODE)+$C$10	=28-E61	=IF(B61<C61,"YES","NO")		
S89	13	14	D	=SUM(B62:C62)	=E62*LOOKUP(D62,CODE)+$C$10	=28-E52	=IF(B62<C62,"YES","NO")		
				TOTAL(£)	=SUM(F18:F62)				
PROPERTIES PER									
LOCATION	NO OF PROPERTIES								
COUNTRY	=COUNT(B18:B24)								
FOREST	=COUNT(B26:B28)								
LAKES	=COUNT(B30:B37)								
MOUNTAIN	=COUNT(B39:B47)								
RIVERS	=COUNT(B49:B53)								
SEA	=COUNT(B55:B62)								
AVERAGE	=AVERAGE(B66:B71)								

Chapter 4, Section 3, Exercise 2

PROPERTY DETAILS				
LOCATION AND PROPERTY CODE	TOTAL WEEKS BOOKED	INCOME	TOTAL WEEKS NOT BOOKED	LOW(A)
COUNTRY				
C181	24	4850.00	4	NO
C34	26	5250.00	2	NO
C66	23	4650.00	5	NO
C670	25	5050.00	3	YES
C777	21	4250.00	7	YES
C91	26	6680.00	2	NO
C997	28	6350.00	0	NO
FOREST				
F129	20	3050.00	8	YES
F642	21	4775.00	7	YES
F919	19	3850.00	9	YES
LAKES				
L654	22	5000.00	6	NO
L67	21	4775.00	7	YES
L801	28	4250.00	0	NO
L802	22	4450.00	6	YES
L816	20	3050.00	8	YES
L817	22	3350.00	6	NO
L855	17	3450.00	11	NO
L919	21	5405.00	7	YES
MOUNTAIN				
M30	20	3050.00	8	YES
M341	20	4050.00	8	YES
M443	20	6050.00	8	YES
M45	15	2300.00	13	NO
M51	23	6950.00	5	NO
M666	20	4050.00	8	YES
M88	21	6350.00	7	YES
M89	20	4050.00	8	NO
M975	28	4250.00	0	NO
RIVERS				
R103	28	8450.00	0	NO
R134	26	5250.00	2	YES
R21	26	5900.00	2	NO
R54	26	5250.00	2	YES
R691	19	3850.00	9	YES
SEA				
S126	23	6950.00	5	YES
S16	21	4775.00	7	YES
S222	26	6680.00	2	NO
S51	28	8450.00	0	NO
S555	24	5450.00	4	YES
S589	24	7250.00	4	NO
S715	24	6170.00	4	NO
S89	27	6935.00	1	YES
	TOTAL(£)	£204,945.00		

Chapter 4, Section 3, Exercise 3

LOCATION AND PROPERTY CODE	PROPERTY DETAILS			LOW(A)
	TOTAL WEEKS BOOKED	INCOME	TOTAL WEEKS NOT BOOKED	
COUNTRY				
C181	=SUM(B18:C18)	=E18*LOOKUP(D18,CODE)+$C$10	=28-E18	=IF(B18<C18,"YES","NO")
C34	=SUM(B19:C19)	=E19*LOOKUP(D19,CODE)+$C$10	=28-E19	=IF(B19<C19,"YES","NO")
C66	=SUM(B20:C20)	=E20*LOOKUP(D20,CODE)+$C$10	=28-E20	=IF(B20<C20,"YES","NO")
C670	=SUM(B21:C21)	=E21*LOOKUP(D21,CODE)+$C$10	=28-E21	=IF(B21<C21,"YES","NO")
C777	=SUM(B22:C22)	=E22*LOOKUP(D22,CODE)+$C$10	=28-E22	=IF(B22<C22,"YES","NO")
C91	=SUM(B23:C23)	=E23*LOOKUP(D23,CODE)+$C$10	=28-E23	=IF(B23<C23,"YES","NO")
C997	=SUM(B24:C24)	=E24*LOOKUP(D24,CODE)+$C$10	=28-E24	=IF(B24<C24,"YES","NO")
FOREST				
F129	=SUM(B26:C26)	=E26*LOOKUP(D26,CODE)+$C$10	=28-E26	=IF(B26<C26,"YES","NO")
F642	=SUM(B27:C27)	=E27*LOOKUP(D27,CODE)+$C$10	=28-E27	=IF(B27<C27,"YES","NO")
F919	=SUM(B28:C28)	=E28*LOOKUP(D28,CODE)+$C$10	=28-E28	=IF(B28<C28,"YES","NO")
LAKES				
L654	=SUM(B30:C30)	=E30*LOOKUP(D30,CODE)+$C$10	=28-E30	=IF(B30<C30,"YES","NO")
L67	=SUM(B31:C31)	=E31*LOOKUP(D31,CODE)+$C$10	=28-E31	=IF(B31<C31,"YES","NO")
L801	=SUM(B32:C32)	=E32*LOOKUP(D32,CODE)+$C$10	=28-E32	=IF(B32<C32,"YES","NO")
L802	=SUM(B33:C33)	=E33*LOOKUP(D33,CODE)+$C$10	=28-E33	=IF(B33<C33,"YES","NO")
L816	=SUM(B34:C34)	=E34*LOOKUP(D34,CODE)+$C$10	=28-E34	=IF(B34<C34,"YES","NO")
L817	=SUM(B35:C35)	=E35*LOOKUP(D35,CODE)+$C$10	=28-E35	=IF(B35<C35,"YES","NO")
L855	=SUM(B36:C36)	=E36*LOOKUP(D36,CODE)+$C$10	=28-E36	=IF(B36<C36,"YES","NO")
L919	=SUM(B37:C37)	=E37*LOOKUP(D37,CODE)+$C$10	=28-E37	=IF(B37<C37,"YES","NO")
MOUNTAIN				
M30	=SUM(B39:C39)	=E39*LOOKUP(D39,CODE)+$C$10	=28-E39	=IF(B39<C39,"YES","NO")
M341	=SUM(B40:C40)	=E40*LOOKUP(D40,CODE)+$C$10	=28-E40	=IF(B40<C40,"YES","NO")
M443	=SUM(B41:C41)	=E41*LOOKUP(D41,CODE)+$C$10	=28-E41	=IF(B41<C41,"YES","NO")
M45	=SUM(B42:C42)	=E42*LOOKUP(D42,CODE)+$C$10	=28-E42	=IF(B42<C42,"YES","NO")
M51	=SUM(B43:C43)	=E43*LOOKUP(D43,CODE)+$C$10	=28-E43	=IF(B43<C43,"YES","NO")
M666	=SUM(B44:C44)	=E44*LOOKUP(D44,CODE)+$C$10	=28-E44	=IF(B44<C44,"YES","NO")
M88	=SUM(B45:C45)	=E45*LOOKUP(D45,CODE)+$C$10	=28-E45	=IF(B45<C45,"YES","NO")
M975	=SUM(B46:C46)	=E46*LOOKUP(D46,CODE)+$C$10	=28-E46	=IF(B46<C46,"YES","NO")
	=SUM(B47:C47)	=E47*LOOKUP(D47,CODE)+$C$10	=28-E47	=IF(B47<C47,"YES","NO")
RIVERS				
R103	=SUM(B49:C49)	=E49*LOOKUP(D49,CODE)+$C$10	=28-E49	=IF(B49<C49,"YES","NO")
R134	=SUM(B50:C50)	=E50*LOOKUP(D50,CODE)+$C$10	=28-E50	=IF(B50<C50,"YES","NO")
R21	=SUM(B51:C51)	=E51*LOOKUP(D51,CODE)+$C$10	=28-E51	=IF(B51<C51,"YES","NO")
R54	=SUM(B52:C52)	=E52*LOOKUP(D52,CODE)+$C$10	=28-E52	=IF(B52<C52,"YES","NO")
R691	=SUM(B53:C53)	=E53*LOOKUP(D53,CODE)+$C$10	=28-E53	=IF(B53<C53,"YES","NO")
SEA				
S126	=SUM(B55:C55)	=E55*LOOKUP(D55,CODE)+$C$10	=28-E55	=IF(B55<C55,"YES","NO")
S16	=SUM(B56:C56)	=E56*LOOKUP(D56,CODE)+$C$10	=28-E56	=IF(B56<C56,"YES","NO")
S222	=SUM(B57:C57)	=E57*LOOKUP(D57,CODE)+$C$10	=28-E57	=IF(B57<C57,"YES","NO")
S51	=SUM(B58:C58)	=E58*LOOKUP(D58,CODE)+$C$10	=28-E58	=IF(B58<C58,"YES","NO")
S555	=SUM(B59:C59)	=E59*LOOKUP(D59,CODE)+$C$10	=28-E59	=IF(B59<C59,"YES","NO")
S589	=SUM(B60:C60)	=E60*LOOKUP(D60,CODE)+$C$10	=28-E60	=IF(B60<C60,"YES","NO")
S715	=SUM(B61:C61)	=E61*LOOKUP(D61,CODE)+$C$10	=28-E61	=IF(B61<C61,"YES","NO")
S89	=SUM(B62:C62)	=E62*LOOKUP(D62,CODE)+$C$10	=28-E62	=IF(B62<C62,"YES","NO")
	TOTAL(£)	=SUM(F18:F62)		

Chapter 4, Section 3, Exercise 5

LOCATION	NO OF PROPERTIES
COUNTRY	7
FOREST	3
LAKES	8
MOUNTAIN	9
RIVERS	5
SEA	8
AVERAGE	7

Chapter 4, Section 3

LOCATION AND PROPERTY CODE	PRICE CODE
COUNTRY	
C670	B
C777	B
FOREST	
F129	A
F642	C
F919	B
LAKES	
L67	C
L802	B
L816	A
L919	D
MOUNTAIN	
M30	A
M341	B
M443	E
M666	B
M88	E
RIVERS	
R134	B
R54	B
R691	B
SEA	
S126	E
S16	C
S555	C
S89	D

Chapter 4, Section 3, Exercise 7

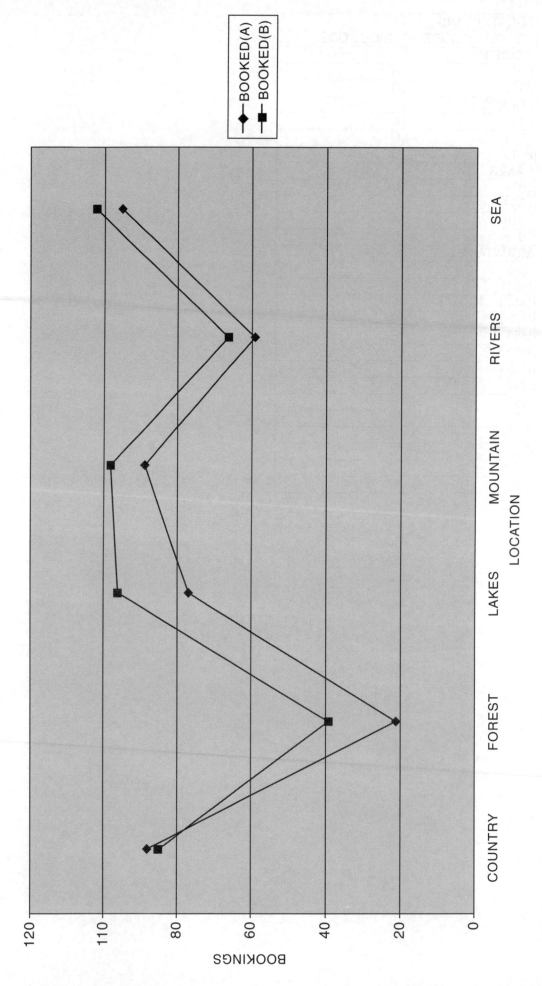

Chapter 4, Section 3, Exercise 8

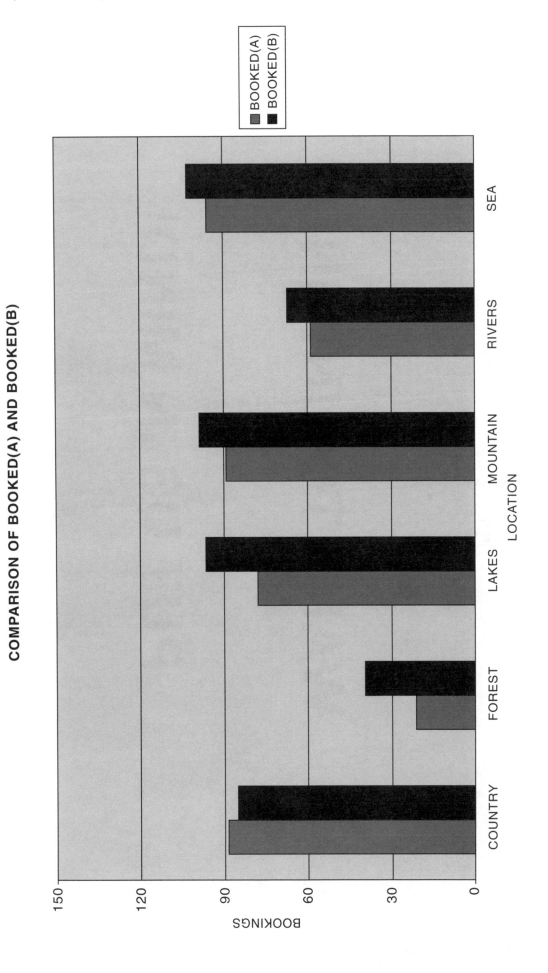

Chapter 5, Section 2, Exercise 9/P5

9 November 1998

WANT TO UNWIND?

PUT US IN MIND!

Angela Bessant

Naturetrail Holidays

Chapter 5, Section 2

NATURETRAIL HOLIDAYS

TOTAL RELAXATION

Tel: 01234 29786

Open 7 to 7

9 November 1998

Angela Bessant

Naturetrail Holidays

Chapter 5, Section 2, Exercise 9/P2

DELIGHTFUL LOCATIONS

Our holiday homes are situated in some of the most beautiful settings, for example:

- Mountains
- Lakes
- Sea

9 November 1998

Angela Bessant

Naturetrail Holidays

Chapter 5, Section 2, Exercise 9/P3

BOOKINGS

Why not take a holiday early in the year when there is usually more choice:

9 November 1998

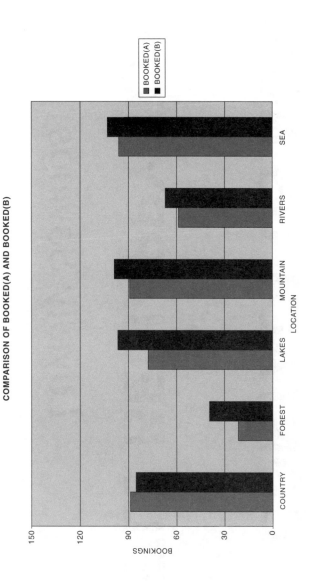

COMPARISON OF BOOKED(A) AND BOOKED(B)

Angela Bessant

Naturetrail Holidays

Chapter 5, Section 2, Exercise 9/P4

CONTACT US NOW!

WE'LL BE HAPPY TO HELP

Loyalty Savings

We will be continuing our loyalty scheme for the foreseeable future and there is also the chance that you may win one of ten super cash prizes.

9 November 1998

Naturetrail Holidays

Angela Bessant

Chapter 5, Section 2, Exercise 9

NATURETRAIL HOLIDAYS

TOTAL RELAXATION

Tel: 01234 29786
Open 7 to 7

Naturetrail Holidays   Angela Bessant   9 November 1998

DELIGHTFUL LOCATIONS

Our holiday homes are situated in some of the most beautiful settings, for example:

* Mountains
* Lakes
* Sea

Naturetrail Holidays   Angela Bessant   9 November 1998

BOOKINGS

Why not take a holiday early in the year when there is usually more choice:

Naturetrail Holidays   Angela Bessant   9 November 1998

CONTACT US NOW!

WE'LL BE HAPPY TO HELP
Loyalty Savings

We will be continuing our loyalty scheme for the foreseeable future and there is also the chance that you may win one of ten super cash prizes.

Naturetrail Holidays   Angela Bessant   9 November 1998

WANT TO UNWIND?

PUT US IN MIND!

Naturetrail Holidays   Angela Bessant   9 November 1998

Chapter 6, Final Publication

19/01/99

Angela Bessant

NATURETRAIL HOLIDAYS

2

If you are looking for a peaceful and relaxing holiday then look no further than Naturetrail Holidays. From small beginnings five years ago when the company had only one location we are now able to offer a choice of six completely different locations. Whatever your idea of the perfect place for a holiday we have the answer.

LOCATIONS

We have holiday cottages in the beautiful unspoilt countryside of the Cotswolds. Here you are able to ramble along the picturesque footpaths and visit the charming villages and small towns that are dotted around this area. Our forest properties are situated in North Wales, close to Betws-y-Coed. There are endless outdoor activities in this area ranging from walking, canoeing or climbing. In Cumbria you will find our lakes cottages - if

you like sailing and fishing then this is the place for you. Again in North Wales, situated in the heart of Snowdonia, you will find our mountain complex. There are even trained mountaineers on hand to give you coaching in all aspects of climbing. So don't worry if you're a novice, there are activities ranging from those for beginners right through to the more experienced climber. Cornwall is the setting for our seaside properties. These are located between Boscastle and Newquay. The scenery in this area is second to none. There are wild coastal footpaths, fishing villages and sandy beaches. You will be spoilt for choice for your daily excursions! For those of you who enjoy the tranquillity of a riverside setting, you will find this at our site in Devon. Our properties are situated only 100 metres from the river Dart. Of course also in this area, in addition to riverside activities, there are beautiful moorland walks.

THE CHOICE IS YOURS. We believe that you cannot fail to appreciate the natural beauty that abounds in all of these locations.

PROPERTIES AVAILABLE

Our properties vary in size and we have properties to suit most needs. You can choose from one to four bedrooms, with the maximum occupancy being eight people (there is the possibility that some of our properties can accommodate babies (cots and high chairs can be provided at no extra cost). Please ask the agent when booking.

PRICES

Prices vary depending on the size of the property. This year we have introduced a new system and now if you book for more than

Angela Bessant

19/01/99

continued

You can arrive on Friday or Saturday depending on which property you have chosen and at any time before 7 pm. Please let us know if you will be arriving later than this. Staggering arrivals in this way makes it easier to ensure that we have more staff available to give you a warm welcome. You may prefer to travel on a Friday, especially in summer when the roads are usually less congested. Whilst on the subject of transport, you will notice that most of our properties have parking adjacent to them. Where this is not the case your vehicle may be left in the parking areas which are never more than 50 metres away. For unloading purposes, parking outside the property is perfectly acceptable but please remember to move your vehicle as soon as you can since it will cause an obstruction.

Your property will have been fully cleaned and inspected before your arrival which can be anytime after 12 noon. All bed linen is provided but you will need to bring your own towels. All properties are self-catering but to help you settle in, we do provide a small grocery basket containing essentials, such as bread and milk. Should you find that things are not to your liking, please contact us straight away. WE PRIDE OURSELVES ON GIVING YOU THE BEST SERVICE AT ALL TIMES.

3

one week, any subsequent weeks are charged at a reduced rate.

The table below shows the prices relating to the different codes:

CODE	COST	EXTRA WEEK
A	£150	£135
B	£200	£185
C	£225	£210
D	£255	£240
E	£300	£285

Why not reserve a property for our early booking period? The properties shown below are on special discount prices (deduct a further 10% from the price shown in the brochure) for this year only:

LOW BOOKINGS PERIOD A	
PROPERTY NAME	**ASPENS**
BOOKED (A)	7
PROPERTY NAME	**HEADLANDS**
BOOKED (A)	7
PROPERTY NAME	**PEANUTS**
BOOKED (A)	7
PROPERTY NAME	**PUFFINS**
BOOKED (A)	5

LOYALTY SAVINGS

Naturetrail Holidays are pleased to announce an important bonus for customers who have taken holidays with us in the past. We are now able to give substantial discounts on your holiday booking this year. If you book your holiday before the end of January you will be entitled to a 20% discount on the standard cost of your chosen property (subject to its availability). If you book before the end of March you will be entitled to a 10% discount on the standard cost.

We feel that this is a very generous offer and hope that you will be able to make your bookings early to benefit from the maximum savings.

Each 'loyalty' customer will be entered into our prize draw. We will be offering cash prizes ranging from £50 to £500 to those lucky ones picked out at random. If you are eligible for this discount please have your

Angela Bessant

19/01/99

continued

> **We will be continuing our loyalty scheme for the foreseeable future and there is also the chance that you may win one of ten super cash prizes.**

19/01/99

4

previous booking reference to hand when you call. If you no longer have your booking reference, don't worry we will be able to look up your details on our database.

HOW TO BOOK

Our properties can be booked from our Head Office by telephoning 01234 29786. We are open from 7 am to 7 pm every day except Sunday. Our regional offices can also help you with any queries that you may have. They are each allocated several properties that are their major concern. Choosing the right accommodation to suit your needs can be difficult and we want to help you make an informed choice. You can rely on our staff giving informative and friendly advice. Our computerised booking system gives instant availability of our properties so that we can suggest an alternative should your first choice be taken. Shown below are the properties dealt with by our Bristol office:

LOCATION	NO OF PROPERTIES
COUNTRY	7
FOREST	3
LAKES	8
MOUNTAIN	9
RIVERS	5
SEA	8
AVERAGE	7

As you can see each regional office deals with properties from all of the locations. Our staff training ensures that all staff have visited the six locations and are aware of the differences between them.

When booking please ensure that you have the following details to hand:

- Reference of Property
- Price Code
- Date Required
- Number in Party
- Vehicle Registration Number
- Credit Card Number
- Former Booking Ref (if applicable)

Here at Naturetrail Holidays we pride ourselves in providing an excellent booking service and we hope that you feel that this level of excellence carries through to all of our operations. We know how important it is that everything runs smoothly so that you are able to relax and enjoy yourselves.

So what are you waiting for? Have another look through our brochure and imagine the fun that you'll have with Naturetrail Holidays.

DON'T DELAY - BOOK TODAY.

Angela Bessant

Full PRACTICE ASSIGNMENT – section B

04/02/99

Query1

PROPERTY NAME	CODE	LOCATION	OCCUPANTS	BEDROOMS	PETS	TV	BOOKED(A)	BOOKED(B)	PRICE CODE	CHANGE DAY	DATE BOOKED	AGENT
ASPENS	M341	MOUNTAIN	2	1	☐	☐	7	13	B	FRI	24-Sep-99	JANE
HEADLANDS	S122	SEA	4	2	☑	☐	7	10	B	SAT	18-Sep-99	PAUL
PEANUTS	F919	FOREST	4	2	☐	☐	7	12	B	SAT	18-Sep-99	PAUL
PUFFINS	S855	SEA	4	1	☐	☐	5	14	B	SAT	25-Sep-99	MIKE

Page 1

Full Practice Assignment – section B

BOOKINGS PERIOD A

PROPERTY NAME	PUFFINS
BOOKED (A)	5
PROPERTY NAME	PEANUTS
BOOKED (A)	7
PROPERTY NAME	HEADLANDS
BOOKED (A)	7
PROPERTY NAME	ASPENS
BOOKED (A)	7

Full Practice Assignment – section B

PROPERTY NAME	LOCATION	BOOKED(A)	PRICE CODE
MARBLE	FOREST	11	C
MISTY	SEA	12	D
MOLLUSCS	SEA	13	D
MUSSELS	SEA	10	C
SEASHORE	SEA	12	E
SHELLFISH	SEA	11	C
SHINGLE	SEA	11	C
SHRIMPS	SEA	7	C
STARFISH	SEA	7	C
SURF	SEA	11	C

Full Practice Assignment – section B

BOOKINGS PER LOCATION

LOCATION	PROPERTY NAME	BOOKED (A)
FOREST		
	MARBLE	11
		11
SEA		
	SURF	11
	STARFISH	7
	SHRIMPS	7
	SHINGLE	11
	SHELLFISH	11
	SEASHORE	12
	MUSSELS	10
	MOLLUSCS	13
	MISTY	12
		94

1

04/02/99

Full Practice Assignment – section C

NATURETRAIL HOLIDAYS										
ANALYSIS OF INCOME										
							BOOKINGS			
			PRICE CODE DETAILS						BOOKED(A)	BOOKED(B)
PRICE CODE		A	B	C	D	E				
COST PER WEEK(£)		150.00	200.00	225.00	255.00	300.00	COUNTRY		88	85
							FOREST		21	39
FIXED CHARGE(£)		50.00					LAKES		77	96
							MOUNTAIN		89	98
							RIVERS		62	66
							SEA		102	112
			PROPERTY DETAILS							

LOCATION AND PROPERTY CODE	BOOKED(A)	BOOKED(B)	PRICE CODE	TOTAL WEEKS BOOKED	INCOME	TOTAL WEEKS NOT BOOKED	LOW(A)			
COUNTRY										
C181	12	12	B	24	4850.00	4	NO			
C34	14	12	B	26	5250.00	2	NO			
C66	14	9	B	23	4650.00	5	NO			
C670	11	14	B	25	5050.00	3	YES			
C777	9	12	B	21	4250.00	7	YES			
C91	14	12	D	26	6680.00	2	NO			
C997	14	14	C	28	6350.00	0	NO			
FOREST										
F129	7	13	A	20	3050.00	8	YES			
F642	7	14	C	21	4775.00	7	YES			
F919	7	12	B	19	3850.00	9	YES			
LAKES										
L654	12	10	C	22	5000.00	6	NO			
L67	7	14	C	21	4775.00	7	YES			
L801	14	14	A	28	4250.00	0	NO			
L802	8	14	B	22	4450.00	6	YES			
L816	7	13	A	20	3050.00	8	YES			
L817	11	11	A	22	3350.00	6	NO			
L855	11	6	B	17	3450.00	11	NO			
L919	7	14	D	21	5405.00	7	YES			
MOUNTAIN										
M30	7	13	A	20	3050.00	8	YES			
M341	7	13	B	20	4050.00	8	YES			
M443	9	11	E	20	6050.00	8	YES			
M45	9	6	A	15	2300.00	13	NO			
M51	14	9	E	23	6950.00	5	NO			
M666	9	11	B	20	4050.00	8	YES			
M88	9	12	E	21	6350.00	7	YES			
M89	11	9	B	20	4050.00	8	NO			
M975	14	14	A	28	4250.00	0	NO			
RIVERS										
R103	14	14	E	28	8450.00	0	NO			
R134	12	14	B	26	5250.00	2	YES			
R21	14	12	C	26	5900.00	2	NO			
R401	10	12	A	22	3350.00	6	YES			
R54	12	14	B	26	5250.00	2	YES			
SEA										
S122	7	12	B	17	3450.00	11	YES			
S126	11	12	E	23	6950.00	5	YES			
S16	7	14	C	21	4775.00	7	YES			
S222	14	12	D	26	6680.00	2	NO			
S51	14	14	E	28	8450.00	0	NO			
S555	10	14	C	24	5450.00	4	YES			
S589	14	10	E	24	7250.00	4	NO			
S715	12	12	D	24	6170.00	4	NO			
S89	13	14	D	27	6935.00	1	YES			
				TOTAL(£)	£207,895.00					

PROPERTIES PER LOCATION										
LOCATION	NO OF PROPERTIES									
COUNTRY	7									
FOREST	3									
LAKES	8									
MOUNTAIN	9									
RIVERS	5									
SEA	9									

Full Practice Assignment – section C

NATURETRAIL HOLIDAYS

ANALYSIS OF INCOME

PRICE CODE DETAILS

	A	B	C	D	E
PRICE CODE	200	225	255	300	
COST PER WEEK(£)	150				
FIXED CHARGE(£)	50				

BOOKINGS

	BOOKED(A)	BOOKED(B)
COUNTRY	=SUM(B18:B24)	=SUM(C18:C24)
FOREST	=SUM(B26:B28)	=SUM(C26:C28)
LAKES	=SUM(B30:B37)	=SUM(C30:C37)
MOUNTAIN	=SUM(B39:B47)	=SUM(C39:C47)
RIVERS	=SUM(B49:B53)	=SUM(C49:C53)
SEA	=SUM(B55:B63)	=SUM(C55:C63)

PROPERTY DETAILS

LOCATION AND PROPERTY CODE	PRICE CODE	BOOKED(B)	BOOKED(A)	TOTAL WEEKS BOOKED (B)	INCOME (C)	TOTAL WEEKS NOT BOOKED (D)	LOW(A) (E)
COUNTRY							
C181	B	12	12	=SUM(B18:C18)	=E18*LOOKUP(D18,CODE,$C$10)	=28-E18	=IF(B18>C18,"YES","NO")
C34	B	12	14	=SUM(B19:C19)	=E19*LOOKUP(D19,CODE,$C$10)	=28-E19	=IF(B19>C19,"YES","NO")
C66	B	9	14	=SUM(B20:C20)	=E20*LOOKUP(D20,CODE,$C$10)	=28-E20	=IF(B20>C20,"YES","NO")
C670	B	14	11	=SUM(B21:C21)	=E21*LOOKUP(D21,CODE,$C$10)	=28-E21	=IF(B21>C21,"YES","NO")
C277	B	12	9	=SUM(B22:C22)	=E22*LOOKUP(D22,CODE,$C$10)	=28-E22	=IF(B22>C22,"YES","NO")
C41	D	12	14	=SUM(B23:C23)	=E23*LOOKUP(D23,CODE,$C$10)	=28-E23	=IF(B23>C23,"YES","NO")
C997	C	14	14	=SUM(B24:C24)	=E24*LOOKUP(D24,CODE,$C$10)	=28-E24	=IF(B24>C24,"YES","NO")
FOREST							
F129	A	13	7	=SUM(B26:C26)	=E26*LOOKUP(D26,CODE,$C$10)	=28-E26	=IF(B26>C26,"YES","NO")
F642	C	14	7	=SUM(B27:C27)	=E27*LOOKUP(D27,CODE,$C$10)	=28-E27	=IF(B27>C27,"YES","NO")
F919	B	12	7	=SUM(B28:C28)	=E28*LOOKUP(D28,CODE,$C$10)	=28-E28	=IF(B28>C28,"YES","NO")
LAKES							
L654	C	10	12	=SUM(B30:C30)	=E30*LOOKUP(D30,CODE,$C$10)	=28-E30	=IF(B30>C30,"YES","NO")
L67	C	14	7	=SUM(B31:C31)	=E31*LOOKUP(D31,CODE,$C$10)	=28-E31	=IF(B31>C31,"YES","NO")
L801	A	14	14	=SUM(B32:C32)	=E32*LOOKUP(D32,CODE,$C$10)	=28-E32	=IF(B32>C32,"YES","NO")
L802	B	8	8	=SUM(B33:C33)	=E33*LOOKUP(D33,CODE,$C$10)	=28-E33	=IF(B33>C33,"YES","NO")
L816	A	13	7	=SUM(B34:C34)	=E34*LOOKUP(D34,CODE,$C$10)	=28-E34	=IF(B34>C34,"YES","NO")
L817	A	11	11	=SUM(B35:C35)	=E35*LOOKUP(D35,CODE,$C$10)	=28-E35	=IF(B35>C35,"YES","NO")
L855	B	6	5	=SUM(B36:C36)	=E36*LOOKUP(D36,CODE,$C$10)	=28-E36	=IF(B36>C36,"YES","NO")
L919	D	14	7	=SUM(B37:C37)	=E37*LOOKUP(D37,CODE,$C$10)	=28-E37	=IF(B37>C37,"YES","NO")
MOUNTAIN							
M30	A	13	7	=SUM(B39:C39)	=E39*LOOKUP(D39,CODE,$C$10)	=28-E39	=IF(B39>C39,"YES","NO")
M341	B	13	7	=SUM(B40:C40)	=E40*LOOKUP(D40,CODE,$C$10)	=28-E40	=IF(B40>C40,"YES","NO")
M443	E	11	9	=SUM(B41:C41)	=E41*LOOKUP(D41,CODE,$C$10)	=28-E41	=IF(B41>C41,"YES","NO")
M45	A	6	9	=SUM(B42:C42)	=E42*LOOKUP(D42,CODE,$C$10)	=28-E42	=IF(B42>C42,"YES","NO")
M51	E	9	14	=SUM(B43:C43)	=E43*LOOKUP(D43,CODE,$C$10)	=28-E43	=IF(B43>C43,"YES","NO")
M666	B	14	9	=SUM(B44:C44)	=E44*LOOKUP(D44,CODE,$C$10)	=28-E44	=IF(B44>C44,"YES","NO")
M88	E	9	9	=SUM(B45:C45)	=E45*LOOKUP(D45,CODE,$C$10)	=28-E45	=IF(B45>C45,"YES","NO")
M89	B	9	11	=SUM(B46:C46)	=E46*LOOKUP(D46,CODE,$C$10)	=28-E46	=IF(B46>C46,"YES","NO")
M975	A	14	14	=SUM(B47:C47)	=E47*LOOKUP(D47,CODE,$C$10)	=28-E47	=IF(B47>C47,"YES","NO")
RIVERS							
R103	E	14	14	=SUM(B49:C49)	=E49*LOOKUP(D49,CODE,$C$10)	=28-E49	=IF(B49>C49,"YES","NO")
R134	C	14	12	=SUM(B50:C50)	=E50*LOOKUP(D50,CODE,$C$10)	=28-E50	=IF(B50>C50,"YES","NO")
R21	C	12	14	=SUM(B51:C51)	=E51*LOOKUP(D51,CODE,$C$10)	=28-E51	=IF(B51>C51,"YES","NO")
R401	A	10	10	=SUM(B52:C52)	=E52*LOOKUP(D52,CODE,$C$10)	=28-E52	=IF(B52>C52,"YES","NO")
R54	B	12	12	=SUM(B53:C53)	=E53*LOOKUP(D53,CODE,$C$10)	=28-E53	=IF(B53>C53,"YES","NO")
SEA							
S122	B	10	7	=SUM(B55:C55)	=E55*LOOKUP(D55,CODE,$C$10)	=28-E55	=IF(B55>C55,"YES","NO")
S126	E	12	11	=SUM(B56:C56)	=E56*LOOKUP(D56,CODE,$C$10)	=28-E56	=IF(B56>C56,"YES","NO")
S16	C	14	7	=SUM(B57:C57)	=E57*LOOKUP(D57,CODE,$C$10)	=28-E57	=IF(B57>C57,"YES","NO")
S222	D	12	14	=SUM(B58:C58)	=E58*LOOKUP(D58,CODE,$C$10)	=28-E58	=IF(B58>C58,"YES","NO")
S51	E	14	12	=SUM(B59:C59)	=E59*LOOKUP(D59,CODE,$C$10)	=28-E59	=IF(B59>C59,"YES","NO")
S555	C	14	14	=SUM(B60:C60)	=E60*LOOKUP(D60,CODE,$C$10)	=28-E60	=IF(B60>C60,"YES","NO")
S589	E	10	14	=SUM(B61:C61)	=E61*LOOKUP(D61,CODE,$C$10)	=28-E61	=IF(B61>C61,"YES","NO")
S715	D	10	12	=SUM(B62:C62)	=E62*LOOKUP(D62,CODE,$C$10)	=28-E62	=IF(B62>C62,"YES","NO")
S99	D	14	13	=SUM(B63:C63)	=E63*LOOKUP(D63,CODE,$C$10)	=28-E63	=IF(B63>C63,"YES","NO")
				TOTAL(£)	=SUMIF(F18:F63)		

PROPERTIES PER LOCATION

LOCATION	NO OF PROPERTIES
COUNTRY	=COUNT(B18:B24)
FOREST	=COUNT(B26:B28)
LAKES	=COUNT(B30:B37)
MOUNTAIN	=COUNT(B39:B47)
RIVERS	=COUNT(B49:B53)
SEA	=COUNT(B55:B63)

Full Practice Assignment – section C

LOCATION AND PROPERTY CODE	TOTAL WEEKS BOOKED	INCOME	TOTAL WEEKS NOT BOOKED	LOW(A)
PROPERTY DETAILS				
COUNTRY				
C181	24	4850.00	4	NO
C34	26	5250.00	2	NO
C66	23	4650.00	5	NO
C670	25	5050.00	3	YES
C777	21	4250.00	7	YES
C91	26	6680.00	2	NO
C997	28	6350.00	0	NO
FOREST				
F129	20	3050.00	8	YES
F642	21	4775.00	7	YES
F919	19	3850.00	9	YES
LAKES				
L654	22	5000.00	6	NO
L67	21	4775.00	7	YES
L801	28	4250.00	0	NO
L802	22	4450.00	6	YES
L816	20	3050.00	8	YES
L817	22	3350.00	6	NO
L855	17	3450.00	11	NO
L919	21	5405.00	7	YES
MOUNTAIN				
M30	20	3050.00	8	YES
M341	20	4050.00	8	YES
M443	20	6050.00	8	YES
M45	15	2300.00	13	NO
M51	23	6950.00	5	NO
M666	20	4050.00	8	YES
M88	21	6350.00	7	YES
M89	20	4050.00	8	NO
M975	28	4250.00	0	NO
RIVERS				
R103	28	8450.00	0	NO
R134	26	5250.00	2	YES
R21	26	5900.00	2	NO
R401	22	3350.00	6	YES
R54	26	5250.00	2	YES
SEA				
S122	17	3450.00	11	YES
S126	23	6950.00	5	YES
S16	21	4775.00	7	YES
S222	26	6680.00	2	NO
S51	28	8450.00	0	NO
S555	24	5450.00	4	YES
S589	24	7250.00	4	NO
S715	24	6170.00	4	NO
S89	27	6935.00	1	YES
	TOTAL(£)	£ 207,895.00		

Full Practice Assignment – section C

LOCATION	NO OF PROPERTIES
COUNTRY	7
FOREST	3
LAKES	8
MOUNTAIN	9
RIVERS	5
SEA	9

Full Practice Assignment – section C

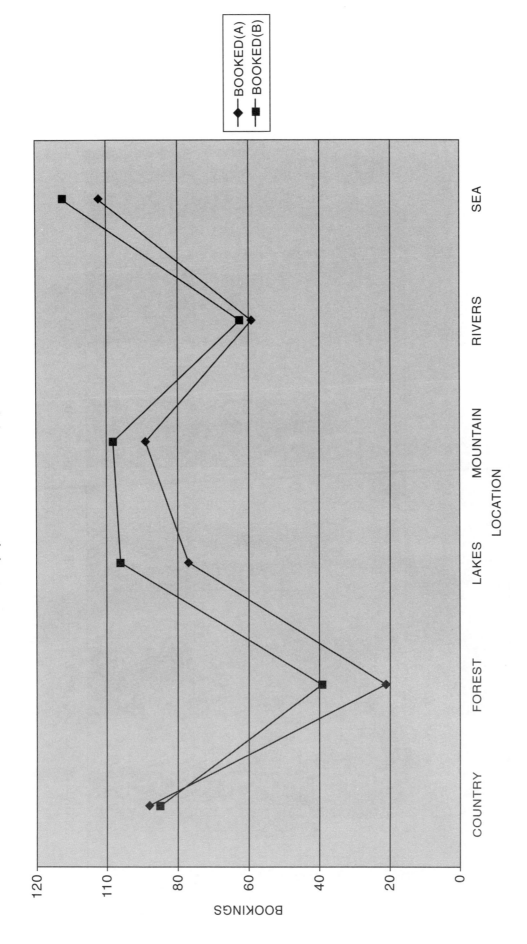

BOOKED(A) AND BOOKED(B) COMPARED

Full Practice Assignment – section C

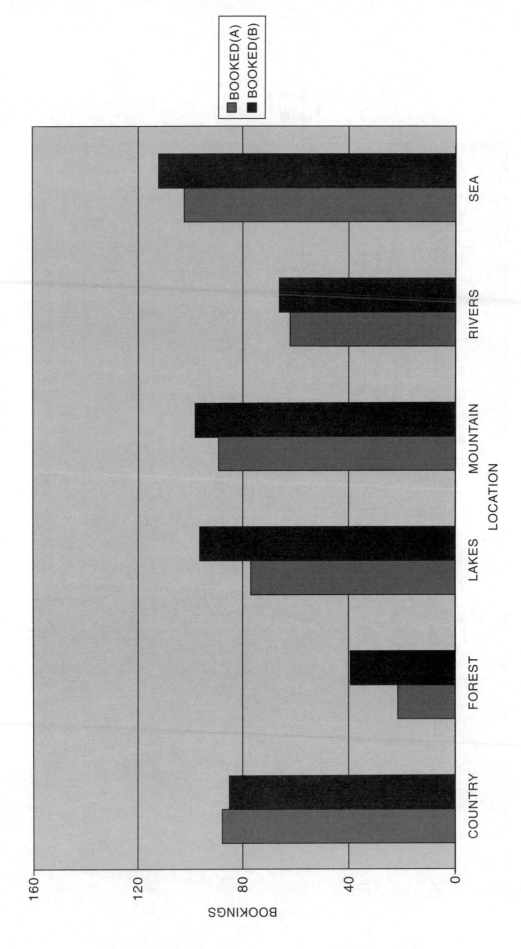

Full Practice Assignment – section C

LOCATION AND PROPERTY CODE	PRICE CODE
COUNTRY	
C670	B
C777	B
FOREST	
F129	A
F642	C
F919	B
LAKES	
L67	C
L802	B
L816	A
L919	D
MOUNTAIN	
M30	A
M341	B
M443	E
M666	B
M88	E
RIVERS	
R134	B
R401	A
R54	B
SEA	
S122	B
S126	E
S16	C
S555	C
S89	D

Full Practice Assignment – section D

Naturetrail Holidays

The Designer

NATURETRAIL HOLIDAYS

TOTAL RELAXATION

The date

Full Practice Assignment – section D

Naturetrail Holidays

The Designer

A PERFECT HOLIDAY

PHONE NOW

Tel: 01234 29786

Open 7 am to 7 pm

The date

Full Practice Assignment – section D

Naturetrail Holidays

The Designer

BEAUTIFUL LOCATIONS

Our holiday homes are situated in some of the most delightful settings, for example:

- *Rivers*
- *Lakes*
- *Sea*
- *Mountains*

The date

Full Practice Assignment – section D

Naturetrail Holidays

The Designer

RESERVATIONS

Why not take a holiday in the spring when there is usually more choice:

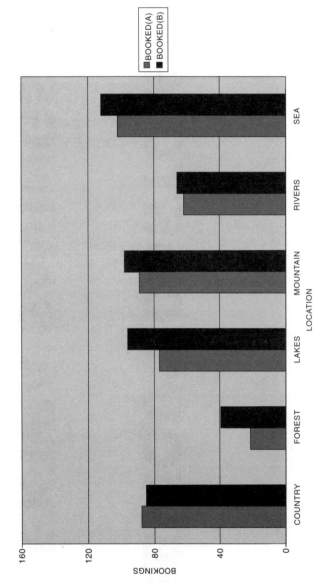

BOOKED(A) AND BOOKED(B) COMPARED

The date

Full Practice Assignment – section D

Naturetrail Holidays

PREVIOUS CUSTOMER?

EXTRA SAVINGS!

Contact us now!

We will be continuing our loyalty scheme for the forseeable future and there is also the chance that you may win one of ten super cash prizes.

Full Practice Assignment – section D

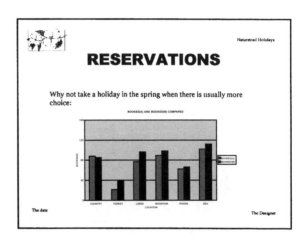

Full Practice Assignment – section D

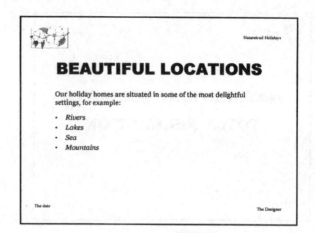

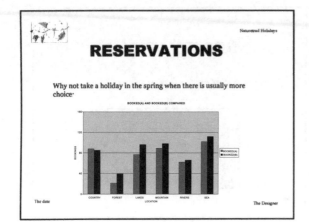

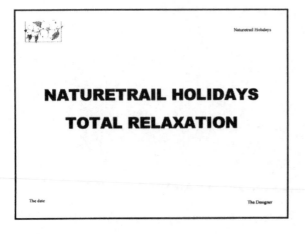

Full Practice Assignment – section F

The Designer

The Date

Full Practice Assignment – section F

2

NATURETRAIL NEWS

If you are looking for a peaceful and relaxing holiday then look no further than Naturetrail Holidays. From small beginnings five years ago when the company had only one location we are now able to offer a choice of six completely different locations. Whatever your idea of the perfect place for a holiday we have the answer.

LOCATIONS

We have holiday cottages in the beautiful unspoilt countryside of the Cotswolds. Here you are able to ramble along the picturesque footpaths and visit the charming villages and small towns that are dotted around this area. Our forest properties are situated in North Wales, close to Betws-y-Coed. There are endless outdoor activities in this area ranging from walking, canoeing or climbing. In Cumbria you will find our lakes cottages - if you like sailing and fishing then this is the place for you. Again in North Wales, situated in the heart of Snowdonia, you will find our mountain complex. There are even trained mountaineers on hand to give you coaching in all aspects of climbing. So don't worry if you're a novice, there are activities ranging from those for beginners right through to the more experienced climber. Cornwall is the setting for our seaside properties. These are located between Boscastle and Newquay. The scenery in this area is second to none. There are wild coastal footpaths, fishing villages and sandy beaches. You will be spoilt for choice for your daily excursions! For those of you who enjoy the tranquillity of a riverside setting you will find this at our site in Devon. Our properties are situated only 100 metres from the river Dart. Of course also in this area, in addition to riverside activities, there are beautiful moorland walks.

THE CHOICE IS YOURS. We believe that you cannot fail to appreciate the natural beauty that abounds in all of these locations.

PROPERTIES AVAILABLE

Our properties vary in size and we have properties to suit most needs. You can choose from one to four bedrooms, with the maximum occupancy being eight people (there is the possibility that some of our properties can accommodate babies (cots and high chairs can be provided at no extra cost). Please ask the agent when booking.

PRICES

Prices vary depending on the size of the property. This year we have introduced a new system and now if you book for more than one week, any subsequent weeks are charged at a reduced rate.

The table below shows the prices relating to the different codes:

CODE	COST WEEK	EXTRA
A	£150	£135
B	£200	£185
C	£225	£210
D	£255	£240
E	£300	£285

Full Practice Assignment – section F (cont'd)

below are on special discount prices (deduct a further 10% from the price shown in the brochure) for this year only:

```
BOOKINGS PERIOD A

PROPERTY NAME    PUFFINS
BOOKED (A)       5
PROPERTY NAME    PEANUTS
BOOKED (A)       7
PROPERTY NAME    HEADLANDS
BOOKED (A)       7
PROPERTY NAME    ASPENS
BOOKED (A)       7
```

You can arrive on Friday or Saturday depending on which property you have chosen and at any time before 7 pm. Please let us know if you will be arriving later than this. Staggering arrivals in this way makes it easier to ensure that we have more staff available to give you a warm welcome. You may prefer to travel on a Friday, especially in summer when the roads are usually less congested. Whilst on the subject of transport, you will notice that most of our properties have parking adjacent to them. Where this is not the case your vehicle may be left in the parking areas which are never more than 50 metres away. For unloading purposes, parking outside the property is perfectly acceptable but please remember to move your vehicle as soon as you can since it will cause an obstruction.

Your property will have been fully cleaned and inspected before your arrival which can be anytime after 12 noon. All bed linen is provided but you will need to bring your own towels. All properties are self-catering but to help you settle in, we do provide a small grocery basket containing essentials, such as bread and milk. Should you find that things are not to your liking, please contact us straight away. WE PRIDE OURSELVES ON GIVING YOU THE BEST SERVICE AT ALL TIMES.

The Designer

3

LOYALTY SAVINGS

Naturetrail Holidays are pleased to announce an important bonus for customers who have taken holidays with us in the past. We are now able to give substantial discounts on your holiday booking this year.

If you book your holiday before the end of January you will be entitled to a 20% discount on the standard cost of your chosen property (subject to its availability). If you book before the end of March you will be entitled to a 10% discount on the standard cost.

We feel that this is a very generous offer and hope that you will be able to make your bookings early to benefit from the maximum savings.

Each 'loyalty' customer will be entered into our prize draw. We will be offering cash prizes ranging from £50 to £500 to those lucky ones picked out at random. If you are eligible for this discount, please have your previous booking reference to hand when you call. If you no longer have your booking reference, don't worry we will be able to look up your details on our database.

HOW TO BOOK

Our properties can be booked from our Head Office by telephoning 01234 29786. We are open from 7 am to 7 pm every day except Sunday. Our regional offices can also help you with any queries that you may have. They are each allocated several properties that are their major concern. Choosing the right accommodation to suit your needs can be difficult and we want to help you make an informed choice. You can rely on our staff giving informative and friendly advice. Our computerised booking system gives instant availability of our properties so that we can suggest an alternative should your first choice be taken. Shown below are the properties dealt with by our Bristol office:

The Date

Full Practice Assignment – section F (cont'd)

LOCATION NO OF PROPERTIES	
COUNTRY	7
FOREST	3
LAKES	8
MOUNTAIN	9
RIVERS	5
SEA	9

As you can see each regional office deals with properties from all of the locations. Our staff training ensures that all staff have visited the six locations and are aware of the differences between them.

When booking please ensure that you have the following details to hand:

- ❑ Reference of Property
- ❑ Price Code
- ❑ Date Required
- ❑ Number in Party
- ❑ Vehicle Registration Number
- ❑ Credit Card Number
- ❑ Former Booking Ref (if applicable)

Here at Naturetrail Holidays we pride ourselves in providing an excellent booking service and we hope that you feel that this level of excellence carries through to all of our operations. We know how important it is that everything runs smoothly so that you are able to relax and enjoy yourselves.

So what are you waiting for? Have another look through our brochure and imagine the fun that you'll have with Naturetrail Holidays.

DON'T DELAY - BOOK TODAY.

Appendix

Changing defaults in Word

Office Assistant

To hide the Office Assistant:
Right-click on the Office Assistant, click on: **Options** and set them to your preferences. Click on: **OK**.

To turn the Office Assistant on:

From the **Help** menu, select: **Show the Office Assistant**

Checking spelling and grammar
There are many options available. Throughout the book, I have chosen to check spelling (not spelling and grammar). I have also chosen not to check on an ongoing basis but after I have keyed in the entire document.

The above settings work well with the students I work with. Should you wish to choose other options: from the **Tools** menu, select: **Options**, and then click on: the **Spelling and Grammar** tab. Select your preferences and click on: **OK**.

Changing the unit of measure
To change the unit of measure from inches to centimetres or vice versa:

1 From the **Tools** menu, select: **Options**, and then select the **General** tab.
2 In the **Measurement** units box, click on: the **down arrow** and then the option you want.
3 Click on: **OK**.

Different types of view in Word

Normal View – this allows for quick and easy text editing.

Print Layout view – this view allows you to see how objects will be positioned on the printed page. It shows margins, headers and footers, and graphics. This is essential for the integrated assignments for IBT III.

File maintenance within programs

In addition to using Explorer, you can carry out file maintenance within programs as follows.

When opening or saving a file, you are able to gain access to your files within the window (figure A.1). This is common to all programs. This window was opened in Word and displays only Word documents (by default). If you want to see other documents, click on: the **down arrow** next to **Files of type** and make your selection.

Figure A.1 Open window

The main shortcut buttons that will be useful for IBT III are shown in Figure A.2. Using these will enable you to find out all the details of your files.

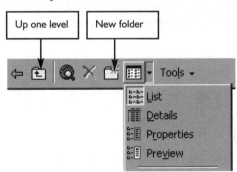

Figure A.2 Shortcut buttons

Right-clicking on a file/folder will bring up the pop-up menu (Figure A.3). This allows you to carry out any of the tasks on the menu.

Figure A.3 File/folder pop-up menu

Adding headers and footers in Excel

1 From the **View** menu, select: **Header and Footer...**
2 The Page Setup dialogue box appears. Click on: the **Header/Footer** tab so that it is displayed as below.

3 Click on: **Custom header**... or **Custom Footer**... .

4 The Header dialogue box appears. Click in the section where you want your name to appear and key in your name. Click in the section where you want the date to appear and key in the date (or click the date button if you are certain that your computer's date is set correctly – the actual date will not be displayed here but you can practise and see what appears on your Print Preview). Click on: **OK**.

A guide to document layout

When you have edited text, or moved text within an exercise, remember adjustment of line spacing is often necessary. When proofreading pay particular attention to line spacing between paragraphs.

When inserting a sentence within a paragraph, make sure the spacing after any punctuation marks remains consistent. Make the necessary adjustments if required.

Use the spellchecker but do realise its limitations.

Line spacing between paragraphs: Press **Enter** twice to leave one clear line space between paragraphs.

Underlining/underscoring: Underlining should not extend beyond the word. For example:

<u>word</u> is correct   <u>word </u>is incorrect

Punctuation

Be consistent with your spacing after punctuation marks. Use the table below as a guide:

Punctuation	Mark	Number of spaces before/after
Comma	,	No space before – one space after
Semi-colon	;	No space before – one space after
Colon	:	No space before – two spaces after
Full stop	.	No space before – two spaces after
Exclamation mark	!	No space before – two spaces after
Question mark	?	No space before – two spaces after

Hyphen: No space is left before or after a hyphen, eg dry-clean.

Dash: One space precedes and follows a dash. Never place a dash at the left-hand margin when it is in the middle of a word or a sentence – always place it at the end of the previous line.

Brackets: No spaces are left between brackets and the words enclosed within them – eg (solely for the purposes of assignments).

Keyboard shortcuts that work (nearly) everywhere

Keyboard	Menu
F1	Help
F7	Tools, Spelling and Grammar
Ctrl + N	File, New
Ctrl + O	File, Open
Ctrl + S	File, Save
F12	File, Save As
Ctrl + W	File, Close
Ctrl + P	File, Print
Alt + F4	File, Exit
Ctrl + X	Edit, Cut
Ctrl + C	Edit, Copy
Ctrl + V	Edit, Paste
Ctrl + Z	Edit, Undo
Ctrl + A	Edit, Select All
Esc	Cancels items

Don't forget! Right-clicking on objects displays pop-up menus in Office 2000.

Integrated Business Technology Technology Stage III. FIT Store Record Sheet

Candidate name _____   _____ *Name of directory created for IBT III project* [   ]

Section	Step no.	Subdirectory	Filename or reference	Query/report name	Tick here*
Prepare source data					
Set up and produce presentation					
Set up and produce publication					

*Tick the boxes if the files saved are to be used later in the assignment.

Time Log Sheet

Section reference	Time started	Time finished	Date	Total time elapsed	Tutor's signature

Candidates should record the section of the assignment worked on and the time they started and finished. On completion of the assignments section a running total should be kept to ensure the total time taken does *not exceed ten hours.*